Lancelot: The Knight of the Cart

Judy with love
from Debbey !

NUMBER XCVII OF THE RECORDS OF CIVILIZATION:
SOURCES AND STUDIES

LANCELOT:
THE KNIGHT of the CART

Chrétien de Troyes

Translated by Deborah Webster Rogers
Introduction by W. T. H. Jackson

COLUMBIA UNIVERSITY PRESS
New York   1984

Library of Congress Cataloging in Publication Data

Chrétien, de Troyes, 12th cent.
Lancelot, the Knight of the carf.

   (Records of civilization, sources and studies; no. 97)
   Translation of: Chevalier de la Charrette.
   Bibliography: p.
   1. Lancelot – Romances. I. Title. II. Series.
PQ1445.L3E5 1984   841'.1   83-23199
ISBN 0-231-05862-4
ISBN 0-231-05863-2 (pbk.)

Columbia University Press
New York   Guildford, Surrey

*Clothbound editions of Columbia University Press books are
Smyth-sewn and printed on permanent and durable acid-free paper.*

To
the memory of my father
K.G.T. Webster

Contents

INTRODUCTION

W.T.H. JACKSON

Chrétien de Troyes was by far the most prolific and influential writer of French narrative poetry in the twelfth century. Of his life nothing definite is known. The appellation "de Troyes" could mean that he was born there or simply that he was connected with the town and, probably, with the court of Champagne.[1] The identification of Chrétien with a certain canon of St. Loup, near Troyes, mentioned in records in 1173, has no supporting evidence, nor has the suggestion that, since Chrétien (Christianus) was a name frequently adopted by converts, he was of Jewish origin.[2]

Since he states expressly that Marie, daughter of Eleanor of Aquitaine, who became countess of Champagne, probably in 1164, had given him the "matière" for *Le Chevalier de la Charrette (Lancelot)*, it seems highly probable that he was acquainted

1. For a carefully reasoned study of the court at Troyes, see J.F. Benton, "The Court of Champagne as a Literary Center," *Speculum* 35 (1961):551-91.

2. The question of Chrétien's possible Jewish origins is raised by U.T. Holmes and Sister M.A. Klenke, *Chrétien de Troyes and the Grail* (Chapel Hill, 1959). The hypothesis has received little support.

with her and hence with her court. The dedication of *Li Contes del Graal* (*Perceval*) to Phillip, count of Flanders, proves no such acquaintanceship but it does indicate that the poem was written before 1190, when Phillip left for the Third Crusade, never to return.

It is fair to assume, from Chrétien's frequent references to Ovid and other classical literature, that he had received a good grounding in the subjects of the *trivium* (grammar, rhetoric, and dialectic), but there is no direct evidence of the equivalent of a university education or of his being a cleric.[3] Nor is it possible to determine where Chrétien gained his knowledge of the Arthurian world. Critics have found evidence in his work of his having read the *Historia regum Britanniae* (History of the kings of Britain) by Geoffrey of Monmouth and Wace's *Brut,* which is based on it, but his treatment of the Arthurian world is so different from that of the historians that it is necessary to postulate "oral tradition" and "lost sources" to explain the different treatment. His works assume knowledge of Arthurian conventions in the audience; otherwise his irony would be lost. Nevertheless, we should never lose sight of the fact that Chrétien's Arthurian romances are the earliest examples of the genre in any language, and that their influence inside and outside France was enormous. It would appear, therefore, that for contemporaries he was the first great exponent of the Arthurian romance and an author of considerable originality. There is little real evidence which would lead a modern critic to challenge that view.

At the beginning of his *Cligès,* Chrétien states that he is the author of *Erec and Enid,* of several French versions of stories

3. The most convenient general account of Chrétien's work is still the chapter by Jean Frappier in R.S. Loomis, ed., *Arthurian Literature in the Middle Ages* (Oxford, 1959), pp. 157-91.

from Ovid, and of "King Mark and Iseut the Fair." Of these only *Erec* is extant. The other works, including that of Mark and Isolde, were probably short poems, like the *Lais* of Marie de France. We can thus be sure that the first two extant romances, *Erec* and *Cligès,* were composed in that order, and that the former was written after 1164, when Marie became countess of Champagne. The next two were *Le Chevalier de la Charrette* and *Yvain.* Many critics believe that Chrétien worked on the two simultaneously, and it is impossible to determine in what order they were made available to the public. Chrétien left the completion of *Le Chevalier de la Charrette* to Godefroi de Lagny, but he did complete *Yvain,* perhaps the best structured of all his Arthurian romances. Chrétien's last work, *Li Contes del Graal (Perceval)* was, as we have seen, begun before 1190 but it was never finished. Godefroi de Lagny, who completed the *Lancelot,* states categorically that he did so with the approval of Chrétien. No such statements are made by the numerous authors who continued *Perceval,* and there is a strong presumption that Chrétien died before he could finish the work.

Although he wrote a few lyric poems, and a narrative poem, *Guillaume d'Angleterre,* is ascribed to him in some manuscripts, Chrétien's fame rests on his romances. It is worth repeating that there is no extant source for any of these romances. The selection of Erec and Yvain to be outstanding heroes at the Arthurian court seems to be Chrétien's own doing, for they are not so singled out in other Arthurian works, except when these are directly dependent on Chrétien's own work. There is no evidence before his poem of any tradition of a love affair between Lancelot and Queen Guinevere and his treatment of the Grail story in *Perceval* differs totally from earlier and contemporary accounts.

Clearly his originality was recognized by contemporaries.

No other French author of the period had so many of his works adapted into other languages, and it is particularly significant that two of the greatest poets who wrote in Middle High German used his work. Hartmann von Aue adapted his *Erec* and wrote a German version of *Yvain* which follows Chrétien's poem in every detail. Wolfram's *Parzival,* although a very different work from *Perceval,* nevertheless stays very close to Chrétien's poem in the material of its narrative — and that in spite of Wolfram's denial that he used the work. In sum we may say that, whatever material was available to him and whatever earlier Arthurian stories he used, Chrétien has a just claim as the originator of the Arthurian romance as a literary genre.

THE ARTHURIAN BACKGROUND

In considering the Arthurian background of Chrétien's romances, it is important to make a clear distinction between the historical, pseudohistorical, and mythological material which is found in them and the conception of an idealized court which provided social and moral standards for Chrétien's heroes and to a large degree controlled their conduct.

The historical material has been thoroughly investigated.[4] The earliest mention of Arthur by name is in a Welsh poem, *Gododdin* (c. 600), where a warrior is praised for his prowess, "even though he was not Arthur." Earlier works, written in Latin, such as that of Gildas (c. 540), and a succession of later authors mention battles and achievements later connected with Arthur, but the first real account of his deeds is given by the

4. See K.H. Jackson, "The Arthur of History," in Loomis, *Arthurian Literature,* chapter 1. There is a convenient collection of the material on the historical Arthur, translated into English in R.L. Brengle, *Arthur, King of Britain* (New York, 1964).

Latin historian Nennius (c. 800). From these scattered fragments of information it seems likely that there was a Welsh chieftain towards the end of the fifth century who put up a spirited resistance to the invading Saxons and who passed into legend as the king who never died but who will come again to revivify his people. The name Artorius was given to this chief. None of the early Latin accounts mentions Queen Guinevere or any of his band of warriors, but in the Welsh prose tale *Culhwch and Olwen* we do find the names of many men who later appear as knights of the Round Table. Here Arthur is a brave and determined king, ready to challenge any odds, but there is no hint of the chivalry which was later to be attributed to his court.

Many critics are of the opinion that the *stories* about Arthur and his warriors were composed largely from Celtic (including Irish) mythological material and that they were transmitted from Wales to Britanny in oral form, since the languages were mutually comprehensible in the early Middle Ages, and were later retold in French by bilingual Breton minstrels.[5] Such an explanation about the spread of Arthurian stories throughout France and even as far as Italy during the eleventh century is perfectly plausible. Certainly many of the names of places and important characters in the romances can be shown to be of Celtic origin and analogues of many of the motifs and individual incidents can be found in Celtic mythology or in Irish saga.[6] But it is dangerous to push these resemblances and analogues too far. Many are of the common stuff of myth, and parallels

5. The standard work on the Celtic origins of the Arthurian stories is R.S. Loomis, *Arthurian Tradition and Chrétien de Troyes* (New York, 1949). Many of the arguments are undeniably strained. For a hostile opinion, see K.O. Brogsitter, *Artusepik* (Stuttgart, 1971).

6. Loomis, *Tradition,* pp. 477f., where some of the strained arguments may be seen.

can be found everywhere, while some of the "identifications" of names rest on the assumption of wholesale distortion, misunderstanding, and careless transmission.

It is significant that there is nothing in extant Celtic literature which could even remotely be called a romance until works appear which are clearly based on French models. The material in the *Mabinogion,* in the *Black Book of Carmarthen,* in the *Book of Taliesin,* and the *Red Book of Hergest,* even though Arthur is mentioned and motifs are found which are like those in Arthurian romance, has none of the characteristics of the romance genre. We must therefore conclude that the early Latin accounts of Arthur and the extant Celtic material do not provide a basis for the treatment of Arthur and his court which we find in the works of Chrétien and his successors. That there was an oral tradition of stories used by minstrels to entertain their audience with Arthurian tales is virtually certain, but it is highly unlikely that these works were romances. It is impossible to say whether they introduced the notion of Arthur's chivalric court, but the possibility seems remote.

It is all the more surprising, therefore, that in 1136 a work was written which offers a totally new view of Arthur's reign. Geoffrey of Monmouth finished his *Historia regum Britanniae* (History of the Kings of Britain) in that year and by 1139 there was a copy of it in the library of a monastery at Bec in Normandy.[7] The work covers the history of Britain from the first eponymous king, Brut, until the death of Cadwallader (689). What is remarkable about the work, however, is that no less than one sixth of it is devoted to the reign of Arthur, and it is clear that its purpose is to glorify both the king and his court and the British, that is to say Celtic, origins of Britain. Geoffrey

7. On Geoffrey, see Loomis, *Arthurian Literature,* chapter 8, by J.J. Parry and R.A. Caldwell.

can be shown to have used Welsh sources, but much of his work is his own invention, as contemporaries such as William of Newburgh pointed out. His *Prophecies of Merlin,* for example, material from which is largely incorporated in the *History,* seems to be largely his own invention, as is the account of the conception of Arthur which has Uther Pendragon disguise himself as the husband of Ygerne. Although sources can be found for some of the accounts of battles described in the *History,* Geoffrey seems to have made up the story of the great climactic battle between Arthur and Lucius Hiberus, emperor of Rome, and, even more important, that of the final battle in which Arthur kills Modred but is mortally wounded himself. This account of the end of Arthur's reign is of great importance. Here we are told for the first time that Modred was the son of Arthur's sister (but not, as later accounts state, that he was Arthur's son), that he took Guinevere in an adulterous "marriage" while acting as governor of Britain in Arthur's absence, that he was killed only after the loss of Gawain and most of Arthur's warriors, that Guinevere went to a convent, and that Arthur was taken to Avalon to cure his wounds. Thus the Welsh tradition of his future return was preserved. It is in Geoffrey's work that we first hear of Guinevere's adultery, transferred by Chrétien to a liaison with Lancelot, whom Geoffrey does not mention.

Geoffrey's work was written as history and as history it was understood by contemporaries and later readers. It was very probably propaganda too, an attempt to counter the extravagant stories which told of Charlemagne's conquest of Britain and which thus gave "authority" to the claims to suzerainty made by French kings. With this intention is connected the most important single feature of the work, its glorification of Arthur's court as the perfection of good manners, courage, loyalty, and civilization. It would be wrong to say that it exhibits the characteristics of what we call "courtliness." The stress is still on war, politics, and conquest, not on love and individual adventure. But the court is the center of civilization and it sets standards. The following passage makes the point clear:

> For at that time Britain was raised to such a pitch of excellence that it far surpassed other kingdoms in manners, in the richness of its material goods, and in the polished behavior of its inhabitants. All the knights who had gained fame by their prowess wore the same colored clothes and arms. The women too were polished in their behavior and also wore the same kind of clothes. They would not accept the love of any knight unless he had proved himself in combat three times. Thus they became chaste and better and the knights showed more prowess in their love for them. After they had refreshed themselves at the feast, they went to the fields outside the city to take part in different sports. The knights devised a game on horseback which gave the impression of a battle while the ladies looked on from the top of the walls. The games stirred their love to a frenzy.[8]

Here, for the first time in connection with Arthur, we have the beginnings of the idea of pleasing a lady by prowess, of the connection between love and adventure and of nobility exalted by love. It is not likely that Geoffrey knew of the new cult of love which was being developed at this time by the lyric poets of southern France, but it is not impossible that he had heard of the cult of love which shortly after is exemplified in the

8. *The Historia Regum Britanniae of Geoffrey of Monmouth,* ed. Action Griscom (London, 1929), pp. 457f.

Roman d'Enéas. However this may be, it is certain that his interest in relations between the sexes at Arthur's court is concerned with manners, not with love.

Geoffrey's work was immensely influential. About 200 manuscripts are still extant and it gained further popularity from the expanded version of Wace, written in Anglo-Norman in 1155, called *Brut*.[9] This is the first work in which the Round Table is mentioned. There is ample evidence that Geoffrey's work was used by other historians and there can be little doubt that Chrétien knew it or a version of it. It is not too much to say that the story of Arthur as the great British king, the counterpart of Alexander and Charlemagne, begins here.

It cannot be overemphasized, however, that Geoffrey's work was intended to be history. Even though later writers of literature used the work, the romances they wrote are totally different in tone. The Arthurian court which makes its first appearance in the romances of Chrétien de Troyes is totally divorced from the realities of history. Although allegedly situated in Britain, its geographical location is uncertain. Knights leave it and go to places in continental Europe without, apparently, ever crossing the Channel. Certain features, such as the Forest of Broceliande, are always near it and seem to represent rather states of mind or locations for a particular type of action than topographical features. Much more important is the fact that inhabitants of the court are always engaged in leisure pursuits. The opening of *Yvain* (the only one of Chrétien's romances which has no prologue) makes it clear that leisure was the normal state of affairs. It is well known that an "aventure," whether in fact or in story, opens every romance except *Perceval,* and so strong did the convention become

9. Wace, *Brut,* ed. L. Arnold (Paris, 1938-40).

that Arthur is frequently shown as refusing to start a feast until an adventure presents itself. It can thus be said justly that Arthur's court exists to give authenticity to adventures. *Perceval* is an exception because the hero actively seeks an identity at Arthur's court, whereas other protagonists already have that identification.

The important characteristic of the Arthurian court is that it has a set of values agreed upon by all its members. None of Chrétien's romances enumerates these values. They are to be deduced from the praise or blame given to the deeds performed, whether that praise or blame comes from the narrator or from other characters. The main concerns of the members of the court are with adventure and the gaining of love, or, in other words, with martial prowess devoted entirely to the honor of the individual and to gaining the affections of a lady with no thought of social considerations other than Arthurian conventions. Marriage is important only as a relationship between two people within which the nature of their love and its relation to other virtues can be tested.

If there were no more to romance than a string of adventures illustrating these qualities, it would hardly be worth serious study. Chrétien and many of his successors used the Arthurian court invented by poets for the manipulation of these qualities and for the evaluation of their usefulness to individuals and to society. Chrétien appears to have decided to use Sir Kei, who in the histories is an honest if unenlightened person, to represent a type of sterile, even brutal, Arthurianism. To him the enforcement of the superficialities of the court is of primary importance, and he regards himself as the supreme arbiter. His effect on Arthur's own conduct is often disastrous, even though the king is well aware of his defects. By his conduct he often drags the court into ignominy and himself acts as a parody of the Arthurian hero.

At the other end of the scale is Gawain. He personifies all that is best in the system. He is gallant, polished, courteous, and kind, the person against whom all others must be measured. Yet he illustrates also the weakness of the Arthurian ethos. His actions are all directed to purely Arthurian objectives and it is only incidentally that he performs acts of humanity, for example, the freeing of the ladies from the Castle of Wonders while he is pursuing the love of Orgeluse. He therefore acts as a foil to such knights as Erec and Yvain who, in different ways, emancipate themselves from the self-centered Arthurian ethos.

All Chrétien's romances are concerned with love. Indeed, it is not impossible that he had a plan to show love in a different way in each of his works, for it is quite certain that Enid's love for Erec bears no resemblance to Laudine's for Yvain or Guinevere's for Lancelot. The courtly convention of love and service to the lady affects all these affairs but they are not merely examples of "courtly love."[10] The term is a nineteenth-century invention and we should beware trying to lump together the love situations in the Provençal *canzon,* the *alba,* and the *pas-*

10. Moshé Lazar, *L'amour courtois et fin'amors dans la littérature du XIIe siècle* (Paris, 1964), gives a good account from the conventional point of view. The concept is seriously questioned by most of the contributions in F.X. Newman, ed., *The Meaning of Courtly Love* (Albany, N.Y., 1968). See D. Kelly, *Chrétien de Troyes: An Analytic Bibliography* (London, 1976) for further studies. In general modern critics try to avoid the expression as too unselective.

torela, all lyric forms, and that which we find in the romance. It is true that in the *canzon* the lady is idealized and that the poet regards the poems he composes to her as love service. But there is never any communication between the poet and his lady, and the whole essence of the genre is that love must be forever in suspense. This is never the situation in the romance, where love is active and progressive, and where the lady, in spite of her great power and her ability to decide the fate of her lover, for good or evil, must obey the rules and grant her love if the knight serves her faithfully and well. Love in the romance does not exist only in the imagination of the lover-persona, as it does in the lyric. Nevertheless, Chrétien makes it very clear that in his Arthurian world, love determines the conduct of both sexes in a manner that would be impossible in the real courts of his day, and that the desire to deserve love and to win it can raise both men and women to heights not otherwise attainable and also lower them to behave despicably.

The triumph of the protagonists over the conventions of the court is what makes the great romances into true works of art. At the beginning the hero acts in accordance with the courtly ethos as he understands it and achieves success. Erec, for example, concerned only with vengeance for the insult offered to him by the black knight and his dwarf takes Enid to the tournament so that he may have a valid "courtly" reason for challenging his opponent. She is at this point no more than an excuse for prowess. But she is also very beautiful and Erec falls in love with her body but not with her. His subsequent neglect of prowess so that he can spend all his time with her shows an Arthurian imbalance which has to be corrected, but the real problem goes deeper. When he hears Enid lamenting his lack of activity, he believes that she is concerned that he is not "honoring" her with knightly prowess. In other words, he judges the event from a purely Arthurian point of view. Nor can we be absolutely sure that such a thought is totally absent from Enid's mind at the time.

Erec determines that she shall have the prowess she desires but that, instead of having the adventures recounted to her, preferably by the knights defeated by her champion, she herself must act as bait for those who are to challenge Erec. If Erec fails her, she will fall prey to those attackers, as indeed she almost does. This perversion of the Arthurian ideal leads Enid and still more Erec to reconsider the whole nature of love and the purpose of adventure, and the final incident, the so-called *Joie de la Cort* episode, shows Erec risking death to free a fellow knight from the slavery to which he has been subjected by a lady who believes that love gives her absolute power over her lover's entire life — a logical extension of the Arthurian ethos.

In *Yvain* too, Chrétien takes care to show how it is possible for a knight to realize that adventure does not exist for the sole purpose of gaining the favor of a lady but to help other women in distress who promise no reward. Yvain returns to his lady after doing long service, not to her but to others, in the guise of the Knight of the Lion. Chrétien leaves it doubtful whether the lady to whom he returns, Laudine, understands or even wishes to understand his motivations.

The progression, then, is away from Arthurian conventions. As the knight leaves the court, returns briefly, and then separates himself completely, so the knight and the lady at first think only in Arthurian terms but end by the recognition of higher values. The same is true of Perceval, who must rise above the ethos of the court before achieving a higher destiny. All three of these romances have a clear two-part structure. In the first part the hero pursues Arthurian ideals and achieves his ends triumphantly. Then follows a catastrophic event which brings about a total change of attitude and action.

It is significant that, in Chrétien's other two romances, the pattern is different. In *Cligès* the first part is about the hero's parents, who are reduced to silence about their perfectly genuine love by the tyranny of court convention and are rescued only by Guinevere's good sense. Their career gives Chrétien the opportunity to indulge in some good natured jesting at the expense of love at Arthur's court. The second part is not so good natured. It is concerned with the attempt of their son, Cligès, to win Fenice, the wife of his father's brother. She will not hear of an adulterous liaison but is quite prepared to use drugs to sham death, to be entombed, recover, and celebrate her union with Cligès in a sepulchre. When they are discovered, they flee to the only safe place, Arthur's court, where they await the death of Fenice's husband. It will be observed that, far from rising above the Arthurian ethos, Cligès and Fenice sink below it and instead of transcending Arthur's court, they take refuge in it. It seems highly probable that, in this work, Chrétien is determined to show how the idea of love could be perverted.

The other romance which does not show a clear two-part structure is *Le Chevalier de la Charrette* or *Lancelot,* and to this we must now turn our attention.

LANCELOT

According to his preface to the work, Chrétien undertook the *Lancelot* at the request of Marie, countess of Champagne, daughter of Eleanor of Aquitaine by her first marriage to Louis VII of France. There is considerable evidence that Marie's court indulged in elaborate discussions of the theory of love and quite possibly in games in which questions concerning love were "tried" in "courts." This interest in love as the center of civilized and particularly of aristocratic life is perhaps what prompted Marie to suggest to Chrétien the story of Lancelot and Guinevere. Where she found the material is not known. There is no extant poem or story about their love which can be dated earlier than Chrétien's romance. In fact, there are no earlier stories in which Lancelot is the hero. The earliest German works, which are not dependent on Chrétien, ascribe numerous adventures with ladies to Lancelot but none of those ladies is Guinevere. It is just possible that Chrétien may have invented the story, but it seems much more likely that Marie gave him at least an outline of it, attracted to it, perhaps, because it represents the ultimate triumph of love over the realities of power. The fate of adulterous queens and courtier-lovers in the Middle Ages and Renaissance is well documented. Adultery was treason and was punished as such. Yet in this poem the king is little better than a cringing figure who cannot guard his own wife, and she is clearly in search of a man of finer stuff and moreover one whom she can dominate while he is capable of dominating everyone else. The Arthurian ethos is here pushed to its logical conclusion: a knight whose love service is the finest imaginable, yet who is the total slave of the lady he serves, a lady whose real desire seems to be to prove her dominance whatever the consequences. There can be little doubt that she corrupts the character of the knight rather than ennobling it and from there it is but a small step to the destruction of the whole Arthurian world which is presented in the Vulgate Version of the Arthurian romances and in Malory's *Morte d'Arthur*. To assert, as C.S. Lewis and others have done,[11] that the love of Lancelot and Guinevere represents the highest

11. C.S. Lewis, *The Allegory of Love* (Oxford, 1936), repr. Oxford University Press, 1958, pp. 23ff.

manifestation of "courtly love" is true only in the sense that it pushes the conventions of that love to extreme limits, indeed to the edge of parody. Before discussing the work any further, it may well be appropriate to summarize the plot.

An unknown knight interrupts the feast Arthur is holding at his court in Camelot on Ascension Day and announces that he holds captive knights and ladies whom he will release only if Arthur entrusts Guinevere to one of his knights, who must then defeat the challenger in battle. If the challenger wins, the queen joins the other captives. Kei tricks the king into giving him the task. He departs with the reluctant queen, and when the king and Gawain ride out they find his horse and broken lance. It is clear that the queen has been abducted. Gawain follows their trail and finds a horse he had lent to Lancelot lying dead. Later he comes on Lancelot himself walking behind a cart. (Lancelot is not named until much later in the poem.) The dwarf who is driving the cart bids him get in if he wants news of the queen. After hesitating two steps, Lancelot does so. He is now riding in the shameful vehicle used to take condemned men to the gallows and he suffers appropriate abuse when passing through a town. Gawain and Lancelot reach a castle where they are well entertained, but Lancelot, though warned of danger, insists on sleeping in the best of three beds, where he is almost killed during the night by a flaming lance. No explanation of the event is given by their hostess the following morning.

As Gawain and Lancelot proceed, they learn that the queen's abductor is Meleagant, son of Baudemaguz, king of Goirre. This land can be reached only by two dangerous bridges, one under the water, one made of sword blades. Lancelot decides to take the road which leads to the sword bridge. On the way there he has to defeat a knight who is guarding a ford. At first he is so lost in thoughts of Guinevere that he is unhorsed but he recovers and wins. He next encounters a lady who will give him lodging and information only if he will lie with her. He reluctantly agrees, rescues her from an "attack" by knights who prove to be members of her own household, and then lies with her only in the most literal sense of the term. She is not offended and agrees to go with him in search of the queen. Next day, he finds a comb with Guinevere's hair and worships it as he would a holy relic. In a cemetery he raises the lid of a tomb destined for him and thereby reveals himself as the liberator of the prisoners in the land of Goirre. After other adventures, Lancelot finally arrives at the sword bridge. On the opposite bank he sees two lions but after he has crawled across and severely slashed his hands and feet, he finds they have disappeared.

Baudemaguz, a kindly man, urges Lancelot to wait until his wounds are healed before fighting, but Lancelot insists on combat the following day. Weakened as he is, he is doing badly until he sees Guinevere watching from a window. Meleagant is saved only by his father's intercession but ungraciously insists on a second combat at Arthur's court.

At their first meeting, Guinevere treats Lancelot, whom she addresses by name, with marked coolness and he leaves. On hearing false reports that she is starving herself to death, he attempts suicide, and she, hearing that he is dead, repents of her anger. Lancelot is brought to see her, and she explains that he had offended her by his hesitation in getting into the cart. That night he comes to her window, forces apart the bars, and their love is consummated. The blood from his hands stains the sheets and the wretched Kei, lying wounded in the room, is accused of adultery. Lancelot now finds himself in the dubious position of defending the innocence of Guinevere and

Kei by fighting Meleagant, whom he again defeats.

Lancelot now sets out in search of Gawain but is ambushed and imprisoned. Gawain has tried to cross by the underwater bridge but he slips off and is rather ignominiously fished out of the water. He learns that the queen has been rescued by Lancelot. A tournament is arranged at Logres at which certain ladies will have an opportunity to choose husbands. Guinevere agrees to attend and is escorted there by Gawain. The wife of the jailor who has Lancelot in prison is so moved by love for him that she agrees to release him to attend the tourney. He fights unrecognized and defeats all comers until Guinevere, believing she recognizes him, sends a message to him that he should lose. He does so, incurring much abuse, until she bids him win, when he carries off all honors. He then loyally returns to his prison. From this he is finally rescued by a damsel to whom he had rendered a service while on the way to the sword bridge and who proves to be Meleagant's sister. She takes him home, nurses him back to health, and keeps him with her until it is time for the combat with Meleagant at Arthur's court. Gawain is prepared to fight in Lancelot's place, but he arrives in time for the combat, fought in an idealized landscape situation near Arthur's court. After a merciless contest, Meleagant is defeated and beheaded, much to the delight of the court.

Several general characteristics may be noted at once. There is in the *Lancelot* no structure which corresponds to that of *Erec* and *Yvain,* and, to a lesser degree, *Perceval*. The hero does not ride forth on a successful adventure, win a lady, and then have the Arthurian world collapse about him. Nor, and this is more important, does he seek a different ethos, a combination of love and prowess directed to higher ends. Lancelot's attitude remains the same throughout. He is devoted to Guinevere with religious fervor, and all his efforts are directed towards serving her. He personifies the most extreme form of the Arthurian love-ethic, even when his devotion makes him betray Arthur. As Tennyson has put it: "Faith unfaithful kept him falsely true." No one can doubt his fanatical devotion and fail to be moved by it, but it is harder to feel sympathy for Guinevere. No one can blame her for the initial abduction, but her almost ruthless exploitation of her power over Lancelot raises serious questions about the nature of the love she feels for him and about the way in which Chrétien wishes us to see Arthurian behavior in the poem. Many critics believe that Chrétien undertook the task imposed on him by Marie de Champagne with great reluctance. Certainly he did not finish the work but handed over the last thousand lines or so to Godefroi de Lagny. His lack of interest may well be part of the reason for the chaotic structure of the poem, especially of the first part. Even the most favorably disposed reader cannot fail to notice the total irrelevance of many of the episodes (for example, the fiery lance) which have no bearing on later events and which the author himself never attempts to explain. Many episodes seem to be little more than an attempt to fill out the work or mark the passage of time. Even incidents which are relevant often seem like duplicates — the amorous jaileress and the amorous sister of Meleagant, for example. The structure too is often clumsy. Why, for example, is there such a long gap between Lancelot's crossing of the sword bridge and Gawain's failure at the underwater bridge?

It is not the structure, then, which gives the poem its reputation. The interest lies in the characters and the tensions between them, their relation to the Arthurian court, and their plight as human beings. There is too the power of Chrétien's poetry to bring them to life.

Lancelot is not introduced into the story as a member of

Arthur's court, nor do we find out who he is until he has performed several deeds. (He is first named in line 3660.) As happens so often in Chrétien's works, the actions which determine his fate in the romance are performed without his participation and even without his knowledge. Yet the events over which he had no control, the challenge to Arthur, the rash boon granted to Kei, the abduction of Guinevere are not the real motivating forces. It soon becomes clear that Lancelot has been in love with Guinevere for some time. His appearance *outside* Arthur's court is therefore more than accidental. For almost the whole poem Lancelot never even visits the court. Only his last combat with Meleagant takes place there, at Arthur's direction, and, it will be remembered, that combat is the direct result of the challenge to the court which opens the poem, not anything to do with Lancelot's love for Guinevere. Although he is regarded as the greatest of Arthur's knights, Lancelot is in this poem an outsider, and in the later works in which he appears he never has the same close relationship to the Arthurian world that is shown by Gawain.

Lancelot's behavior in love is also worth consideration. We do not see him fall in love, as we do Erec, Cligès, and especially Yvain. There is no opportunity for us to observe the first impact on him of Guinevere's beauty—nor for Chrétien to treat us to the Ovidian symptoms of the love-disease. He is already in love when we first encounter him but only gradually do we become aware of the fact. The most telling incident is the finding of the comb with the queen's hair entangled in it. The scene is strongly reminiscent of the episode in *Cligès* where Alexander discovers that Sordamors has sewn one of her long blond hairs into his shirt and spends the night hugging and kissing a shirt. Yet the scene in *Cligès* is so treated that the reader must find it comic, whereas Lancelot's intensity of passion is clearly to be linked with mysticism and religious devotion. To Lancelot, the hair has all the power of a saint's relic, but the reader is left with the uneasy feeling that perhaps there is a similarity between his behavior and that of Alexander.

Lancelot's devotion is absolute. He dedicates himself entirely to the service of Guinevere, even if that means death or, still worse, dishonor. His love service, in other words, is not the fulfilling of an Arthurian convention but of his own inward drive. Here, and in many other respects, he is like Tristan, and it seems that Chrétien borrowed freely from the Tristan story, which he mentions in *Cligès*.

Lancelot is like Tristan too in his sensual desires. In all the romances, the consummation of love is important, but in no other story of Chrétien's is it accompanied by such images of love and violence as in the *Lancelot*. The slashing of hands and feet, the tearing apart of window bars, the blood on the sheets are typical.

Thus there is a sharp contrast between Lancelot's love and that of the Arthurian convention. His love is individual, even fanatical. Although it may conform outwardly to some of the practices of the Arthurian court, it is really opposed to them, for it has no positive social purpose. If it continues its course (a question left open by Chrétien), its only result will be to shatter the Arthurian world, as it does in later versions.

In assessing the role of Lancelot, it is useful to compare him with Gawain. Indeed, it seems that Chrétien intended us to do so. Gawain is present when the challenge is made, but Kei deprives him of any opportunity to take it up. He does the next best thing. He goes out to track the queen and her abductor and accompanies Lancelot when he finds him. Typically, he attempts the sensible crossing of the water by the submerged bridge, and, in spite of a gallant attempt, fails. His only important action is to accompany the queen to the tournament at Logres. He follows a pattern found in many romances when he offers to take the place of his friend Lancelot in combat, but he is not called upon to do so. Throughout, Gawain behaves impeccably by Arthurian standards but he achieves nothing. His role in the romance genre as the touchstone by which other knights are judged is well known. It is most prominent in *Perceval* but it is very important in *Erec and Enid* too. In the *Lancelot,* it appears as if this role has been deliberately diluted. The friendship between Lancelot and Gawain is deep and sincere, but the feeling persists that, if Gawain was the best the court had to offer, it would not be difficult for Lancelot to surpass him.

If the stature of Gawain is much diminished in comparison with the figure we find in other romances, the figure of Arthur suffers still more. When he should be paying close attention to the challenge to his court and his person, he allows his attention to be diverted by Kei and is so desperately anxious to keep him at court that he allows himself to be tricked into naming Kei as Guinevere's escort. Nor does he himself make any serious effort to recover her. Only at the end of the poem does he revert to his customary role as a courteous master of ceremonies for a judicial combat. This was the role he played in *Erec,* but in that poem he was not faced by the personal challenge we find in the *Lancelot.* It is a commonplace of Arthurian criticism that all the romances play down the role of Arthur so that the protagonist — Erec, Yvain, Lancelot, Perceval — may appear to greater advantage. Here we may legitimately ask whether Chrétien has not lowered the stature of the king still more because of the involvement of the hero with the king's wife and lowered the stature of the court for the purpose of ironical criticism of its conventions.

The author's treatment of Kei seems to support this point of view. As we have seen, he was a bold and noble knight in the chronicles. In *Erec* and *Cligès,* his role, though not distinguished, does not make him into the coarse, ill-tempered, and even dangerous boor that we find in *Yvain* and *Perceval,* where his actions bring misery and even death to innocent people. It would appear that, in *Lancelot,* Chrétien is introducing him as the lowest representative of Arthurian values. Here his greatest fault is arrogance, reinforced with complacency. His insistence on recognition as champion of the court leads not only to the abduction of Guinevere but also to the adultery between her and Lancelot, for it is hard to believe it would have happened if she had been escorted by a better champion — or not abducted at all. It is not, therefore, unjust that, wounded though he is, Kei should be charged with adultery, and this fact is one more piece of evidence of Chrétien's ironical intent.

The role of Guinevere is subject to various interpretations. As we have pointed out, she enters into an adulterous "marriage" with Modred in the work of Geoffrey of Monmouth, but it is hard to determine the degree of her guilt. In Chrétien's other romances she is very much the arbiter of matters concerned with love at court, but there is no hint of disloyalty to Arthur. Even at the beginning of the *Lancelot,* she begs Arthur to keep Kei but she is most unwilling to leave the court. Her subsequent actions could be regarded as motivated by disgust at Arthur's weakness, but this is not likely. Lancelot's love hardly seems to come as a surprise to her, for she would scarcely be offended at his hesitation in getting into the cart if she did not know of his love. Even after the consummation of their love, Guinevere's main purpose is to demonstrate her power over Lancelot — to show it off in the conventional Arthurian form: the knight's act of love service. Her message to him to fight badly has been explained as no more than a desire to find out that the knight really was Lancelot, but, if this were so, there would be no need for the farce to continue as it does. Guinevere's desire for power is stressed far more strongly by Chrétien than by others who treat the story, and this leads to the suspicion that Chrétien was here showing what happens to individuals and society when the Arthurian convention is pushed to its limits.

If one regards Guinevere, as one must regard Lancelot, as a victim of overwhelming passion, then her actions are easily explained. But all the evidence is against such an interpretation. She is always too calculating and can keep a suitable distance between her actions and any passion she may feel. She does not appear to be moved by any question of disloyalty to Arthur nor has she any hesitation in returning to court, where her affair must cease or produce a major disruption.

At the end of the work, Arthurian order has been restored. The queen and the knights are back at court, the violent intruder has been defeated and killed. Yet the reader knows that this "harmony" is a sham. Here, as so often, we must note the difference between *Lancelot* and *Erec* and *Yvain*. In the latter romances, the protagonists are different people with different values, even though the court is unchanged. There is no evidence that Lancelot and Guinevere are changed people, except that they have committed adultery, and what their future is, we do not know. Was this vagueness Chrétien's intention? Or did he mean that the Arthurian system solved nothing? The question is fascinating and insoluble. *Lancelot* remains the most enigmatic of Chrétien's romances.

THE TRANSMISSION OF THE POEM

Le Chevalier de la Charrette is found in six manuscripts, of which by far the most important is Bibliothèque Nationale, français, 794, usually called, after its scribe, the Guiot manuscript. It is of the thirteenth century. The other five are less reliable and in some cases have gaps in the text. In the Guiot manuscript, *Lancelot* appears between *Erec* and *Cligés*. It has no title, and the first indication of the name of the author is the mention of him in the text. Full details of the manuscripts are given in Foerster's edition (see below).

The standard edition of the poem is to be found in Wendelin Foerster, *Christian von Troyes, Sämtliche Werke,* vol. 4, Karren-ritter und Wilhelmsleben (Halle, 1899). Although the edition takes note of readings from all the manuscripts, it is generally agreed that it is far from being a complete critical edition. More generally useful is Mario Roques, *Les Romans de Chrétien de Troyes,* vol. 3, *Le Chevalier de la Charrete* (Paris: Champion, 1958), which is based on the Guiot manuscript.

REMARKS ON THE TRANSLATION

Chrétien de Troyes wrote bad English. Several characteristics of his style I have simply silently changed.

Verb tenses: Chrétien keeps shifting between past and present, and sometimes future. This is useful for rhyme and meter, and scarcely bothers hearers. For readers, I have kept it nearly all in the past.

Pronouns: for Chrétien's "he" (usually "cil"), I freely substitute "the knight" or whatever makes the passage clear. Of course I do not use a name unless Chrétien has already used it.

Doubled words: Chrétien often uses two synonyms, which is fine for his verse but pointless and slow in prose. I often, not always, reduce them to one (e.g., l. 3579, "en orisons et en proixeres," rendered as "praying").

Litotes: Chrétien often uses a negative construction to convey a positive meaning. My listening colleague became so confused and annoyed that I have changed some of these to a simple positive.

This translation is based on the Roques edition of the Guiot manuscript. Line numbers from this edition have been inserted in brackets in my translation.

Deborah Webster Rogers

LANCELOT:
THE KNIGHT OF THE CART

SINCE my Lady of Champagne wants me to take up romance-writing, I will do it gladly, as a liege man who will serve her to the limit of his ability, without wasting time on flattery. A writer who wanted to flatter her might say — and I would back him up — that this lady surpasses all other ladies alive as the May zephyr surpasses all other winds. Indeed, I'm no man to use flattery on his lady. Shall I say, "As many sardonyx and semiprecious stones as a diamond is worth, the Countess is worth so many queens"? Not at all: I'll say nothing of the kind — but whether I say it or not, it's true.

This I will say: her command does more for this story than any thought or labor of mine.

Of *The Knight in the Cart* Chrétien here begins his book. The material and the theme have been presented to him by the Countess. He has set the story in order, adding only his labor and understanding of it, as follows.

Once upon an Ascension Day, King Arthur was holding court as sumptuously as he liked, as richly as befitted a king. After dining he did not leave his companions; there were many lords in the hall, and also the Queen, and with them, I believe, many fair and courteous ladies, conversing in beautiful French.

Kay, who had been serving the tables, was eating with the other attendants. And where he was sitting a knight appeared, arriving at the court elegantly equipped and fully armed.

Thus he walked up to the King seated among his lords and with no greeting began, "King Arthur, I hold in captivity knights, ladies, and maidens of your land and your very household. I'm not bringing you news of them because I plan to give them back; rather, I'm letting you know that not all your strength nor all your riches can win them. Know that you'll die before you can help them."

The King answered that if he could not right the matter, he would have to endure it, heavily though it grieved him.

The knight made as if to leave: turned away and did not linger before the King. He reached the hall door, but did not go down the steps; instead, he stopped and cried from there, "King, if there's one knight at your court whom you'd dare trust with the Queen, to escort her into this forest on my track, I will pledge myself to wait for him there, and to return all your prisoners from my land, if he can defend her against me well enough to bring her back here."

Many people in the palace heard him; the court was buzzing with it. Kay too heard the news, where he was eating with the servers. He left his meal, came straight to the King, and began in a good-natured tone, "Sire, I have served you most faithfully and loyally. Now I will take my leave and go away and never serve you again: from now on I have no more wish or desire for your service."

The King was distressed to hear that, but answered as best he could, promptly asking Kay, "Is this serious, or are you joking?"

And Kay answered, "Your Majesty, I am not your jester. I

am taking my leave in sober earnest. I ask no more wages [100] for my service; I have simply decided to leave at once."

"Is it for anger, or because you've been offended, that you want to leave? Seneschal, be at my court as you've always been. Know that there is nothing in the world I wouldn't give you right away, if you will stay."

"Sire, it's no good. I wouldn't take a pound of pure gold a day."

The King in despair went to the Queen. "Lady," he said, "do you know what the Seneschal is asking me? He wants leave to go, and says he'll never live at my court again, and I don't know why. What he won't do for me, he'll quickly do if you ask him; go to him, my dear lady, if he won't deign to stay for me. Beg him for your sake — fall at his feet, rather than let him go. For I'd never be happy again if I lost his company."

Dispatched by the King, the Queen went to the Seneschal. She found him with the others and when she reached him, said, "Kay, you must know that this is most unwelcome news I hear about you. They say, to my distress, that you want to leave the King. Wherever did you get that idea? I don't find you wise or courteous at all, as I have till now. I would beg you to stay: Kay, stay here, please; I ask it."

"Lady, thank you, but I'm not staying."

And the Queen begged him again, and all the other knights at once; and Kay said she was wasting her efforts.

The Queen, from her full height, fell at his feet.

Kay begged her to get up, but she refused: she would never rise until he granted her request.

Then Kay promised to stay, provided the King would grant him what he wanted. And the Queen herself pledged the royal word: "Kay, whatever it may be, both he and I grant it. Now come, and we'll tell him you're staying."

Kay went with her to the King. "Sire," she said, "I've kept Kay, with great difficulty; but I've bound him to you with a promise that you will do whatever he asks."

The King heaved a sigh of relief and said he would do Kay's bidding, whatever he requested.

"Sire," answered Kay, "learn what I want, what the boon is which you have pledged me. I count myself very fortunate to get it, and I thank you. You have promised to give the Queen here into my keeping, and we will go after that knight waiting for us in the wood."

This dismayed the King, yet he did give her into Kay's charge, for he had never once gone back on a promise. But he did it in anger and sorrow, which showed in his face.

The Queen too was dismayed. Everyone in the house said Kay's request was pride, outrage, and insanity.

The King took her by the hand and said, "Lady, incontestably, you must go with Kay."

And he said, "Entrust her to me and don't worry about a thing; I'll bring her back all safe and sound."

Arthur handed her over and Kay escorted her away. Everyone poured out after the pair, and not one but was indignant. Know that the Seneschal [200] was all armed, and his horse was led into the middle of the courtyard, and beside it a palfrey fit for a queen, neither restive nor hard-mouthed.

Downcast, sorrowful, and sighing, the Queen came to the palfrey and mounted, murmuring softly so as not to be heard, "Ah, King [possibly Ah, my dear], if you knew about this, I don't believe you would let Kay escort me one step." She thought she had spoken very low, but Count Guinables heard her, who was nearby when she mounted.

As she departed, everyone who heard mourned as though she lay dead on her bier. They never expected her back in her lifetime.

The Seneschal, in his overweening pride, was leading her to where the other knight awaited them. But no one was concerned enough to follow them, until Lord Gawain said quietly to his uncle, "Sir, you've done something extremely childish. I'm surprised. But if you'll take my suggestion, while they're still so close, you and I shall go after them, and anyone else who wants. I couldn't stop myself from going quickly: it would be wrong not to follow, at least till we know what will become of the Queen and how Kay will fight."

"Let's go, dear nephew," answered the King. "That's a courteous suggestion.[1] Since you've undertaken the matter, have the horses brought out, bridled, and saddled so that we have nothing left but to mount."

At once the horses were produced and saddled. First the King mounted, then Lord Gawain, and all the rest as fast as they could. Everybody wanted to join, and everyone rode off as he wished: armed, some of them, and also plenty without arms. Sir Gawain was armed, and had two squires with chargers led at their right hand.

Approaching the wood, they saw Kay's horse coming out, recognized it, and saw both reins were broken off the bit. The horse was coming home all alone. Its harness was bloody and

1. "Extremely childish" — "Courteous suggestion." Arthur sounds over-patient; presumably, he is so concerned about Guinevere that he overlooks Gawain's sharp words in his relief at his nephew's taking action.

the cantle burst. Everyone who saw it was upset, and they pointed and nudged each other.

Sir Gawain, riding far ahead of the crowd, soon sighted another knight riding at a walk, on an exhausted, sorry horse, panting and sweating. The knight greeted Gawain first, and then Lord Gawain him. He stopped, recognizing Gawain, and said, "Sir, don't you notice that my horse is lathered and no more use? I think these horses are yours; I would beg you — under promise of returning the favor — to lend or give me one of them, whichever."

And Gawain answered, "Choose whichever you prefer."

The other knight, in great need, did not go picking the better, the handsomer, nor the larger. He simply swung into the saddle of the horse he found nearer him and took off at a gallop. The horse he had left dropped dead, for that day he had worked it to exhaustion.

Without a pause the knight, fully armed, rode off through the forest, [300] and Sir Gawain chased madly after him down a hill. After a long ride, he found the horse dead which he had given the other knight, and saw a large area of hoofprints, with many fragments of shields and lances around. It looked as if there had been a hard fight by several knights, and Gawain was very sorry not to have been there.

He did not tarry long, but hurried on, until he came upon the other knight alone, on foot, fully armed: helmet laced, shield on neck, and sword belted. He had come up with a cart.

Now a cart, in those days, was used as a pillory is in ours. In every good town, where we have more than three thousand, they had only one common to them all, the way pillories are, for murderers or criminals, those who have lost an ordeal by combat, burglars or highwaymen. Anyone caught in a crime was put on the cart and led through the streets. He had lost all honor and could never be heard, honored, or welcomed at court. Because carts were so painful in those days the proverb arose, "When you see or meet a cart, cross yourself and remember God, lest ill befall you."

The knight on foot, with no lance, went after the cart and saw a dwarf on the shafts, holding a long switch in his hand, like a carter. The knight said, "Dwarf, for God's sake, tell me if you've seen my lady the Queen pass this way."

That low, base dwarf would tell him no news, but only said, "If you're willing to get into the cart I'm driving, you can find out by tomorrow what's become of the Queen."

At first, the knight kept on walking without getting in. That was his unlucky day, an ill-omened shame, which kept him from jumping in at once. He will feel ill-used because of this. But Reason, which disagrees with Love, warned him not to get in, scolded him, and counseled him to get involved in nothing which might bring him shame or reproach. It was not in his heart, only in his mouth, this Reason which dared talk so. But Love was inside his heart, commanding him to get right into the cart. Love willed it: in he jumped, not caring about the disgrace, for these were Love's orders and desires.

Lord Gawain spurred along after the cart. When he found the knight sitting there, he was surprised. Then "Dwarf," he said, "tell me about the Queen, if you know."

The dwarf answered, "If you hate yourself as much as this knight sitting here, get in with him, if you care to, and I'll drive you along with him."

Hearing that, Sir Gawain took it for sheer insanity and said he would never get in. That would be too base a trade, his horse for a cart. "But go wherever you want, and I will follow."

So they set off, one on horseback and two on the cart, by a single road. Late in the evening they reached a castle, [400] very rich and beautiful. All three entered through a gate.

At the knight's arrival in the dwarf's cart, the people were astonished, and did not just murmur about it: rather, they hooted it through the streets, great and small, old and young. The knight heard plenty of insults and slander. Everyone was asking, "What torture will that knight get? Will he be flayed? Hanged? Drowned? Burnt on a thorn-fire? Tell us, dwarf, you're driving him, tell us, what crime was he caught in? Has he been found guilty of theft? Is he a murderer? Did he lose an ordeal by combat?"

The dwarf just kept his mouth shut, with neither yea nor nay. He drove the knight toward a lodging, and Gawain followed, straight toward a tower situated on the same level as the village. There were meadows on one side and on the other the tower, on a dark rock, high and sheer.[2] Gawain entered on horseback, behind the cart.

In the hall they met a beautifully dressed maiden, the loveliest in the region; and they saw two other girls accompanying her, beautiful and well-bred. As soon as they saw Lord Gawain, they greeted and made much of him. And about the other knight, they asked, "Dwarf, what has this knight done wrong, whom you're driving, helpless?"

The dwarf would give no explanation: he just made the knight get off the cart and left. They did not know where he went.

Sir Gawain dismounted, and two servants advanced and disarmed both knights. The damsel had two fur gowns

---

2. "On the same level" — "high and sheer." The topography Chrétien describes seems to be a scarp. The cart has driven on one level across fields, through a gated wall, through a village, and to the tower; the opposite face of the tower continues the face of a cliff, which drops into the valley where they see the Queen ride by the next day.

brought, which they put on. At supper time the meal was nicely served, the maiden sitting next to Sir Gawain. The knights had no desire to change lodgings or look for better, for she gave them great honor and excellent company all evening.

After they had eaten enough, two beds, high and long, were made up in a room; and there was also a third, more beautiful and rich than those. The story says it had all the luxury imaginable in a bed. When the time and place came to retire, the maiden led both her guests to their room. Showing them the two fine, long, wide beds, she said, "These beds in front are made up for you; but in that bed beyond, no one lies who hasn't earned it. That one wasn't made for you people."

The knight answered — the one who arrived in the cart, feeling offended and insulted by the damsel's prohibition — "Tell me the reason that bed is forbidden."

She answered roundly what had been in her mind: "It's not for the likes of you to ask. A knight is shamed through the whole world if he's been in a cart, and it's not right for him to mix in what you asked me about, and specially to lie there; he'd soon pay for it. I didn't have it so richly made up for you to lie in. If you went any further than thinking about it, you'd pay dearly."

"That you will see when the time comes," he retorted.

"I'll see?"

"Indeed."

"That remains to be seen."

"I don't know about paying," said the knight, "but by my head, whoever is angered or whoever is grieved, I intend to lie in that bed [500] and rest at my ease."

After taking off his shoes, he got into the bed, which was longer and higher than the others by half an ell each way. Down he lay on a yellow samite coverlet starred with gold.

And there was nothing mangy about the fur: it was sable. His covers were fit for a king; and the mattress was not of thatch nor straw nor old matting, either.

At midnight from the rafters fell a lance like a lightning-bolt, point down, as if to pin the knight through the flanks to the coverlet and white sheets and mattress he was lying on. The lance's pennant was all of flame; the fire kindled the cover, the sheets, and the mattress together. And the point passed so close to the knight's side that it nicked off a shaving of skin, but did not draw blood.

He sat up, put out the fire, took the lance and flung it into the middle of the room, all without leaving his bed. Then he lay back and slept as peacefully as before.

The next morning at sunrise, the damsel of the tower was having Mass said for them, so she had them roused. When Mass was sung, the preoccupied knight, he who had ridden in the cart, walked to the windows which overlooked the fields and gazed down along them. The maiden had come to the next window, and Lord Gawain had engaged her in a quiet tête-à-tête, I don't know on what. I have no idea what they were talking about; but as they leaned from the window, they saw, down beyond the meadows along the riverbank, a stretcher being carried, with a knight on it, and great sorrow and mourning by three damsels alongside. After the bier they saw a crowd following, led by a tall knight escorting a beautiful lady at his left.

The knight in the window recognized her as the Queen. He gazed and gazed at her, plunged in contemplation, delighted at the sight, as long as he could gaze. And when he lost sight of her, he was about to let himself overbalance and fall clear to the ground. He was half out the window when Lord Gawain saw him, hauled him back, and said, "Mercy, Sir, take it easy!

For Heaven's sake don't even think of doing youself such harm. You are quite wrong to hate your life."[3]

"But he's right," put in the girl. "Won't everybody hear the news of his misfortune, that he's been in a cart? He certainly ought to prefer being killed: he's better dead than alive. His life from now on is shameful, contemptible, and unhappy."

The knights asked for their arms and donned them. And then the damsel dealt courteously and nobly with them, and generously: after she had sufficiently teased and mocked the knight, she gave him a horse and lance, for friendship and atonement. The knights took leave of her politely, said good-bye, and rode off as the path led them, leaving the castle in such a way as to avoid being spoken to. They rode quickly in the direction where they had seen the Queen, [600] but did not overtake the cortège, though they were galloping.

From the fields, they rode through a hedge and found a paved road, on which they wandered through the forest until maybe Prime,[4] when they met a damsel at a crossroads. Both greeted her and asked her — begged her — to tell them (if she knew) which way the Queen had been led.

She answered sensibly, "You could certainly promise me enough for me to set you on the right road and name you the country and the knight who is taking her. But there will be great hardship for anyone who wants to enter that land: before he got in, he would have great pain."

3. "Hate your life." Peace to Gawain and even Douglas Kelly, this is *not* a suicide attempt. Lancelot's intention is not to kill himself, but *to keep the Queen in view*. That continuing to watch her will make his body overbalance is the farthest thing from his awareness — compare his stupor at the ford, with the comb, and during his first fight with Meleagant.

4. "Prime." The canonical hours were Matins, celebrated at or about midnight, Lauds around 3 A.M. (or dawn), Prime around 6 A.M., Tierce 9 A.M., Sext at midday, Nones 3 P.M., Vespers 6 P.M., Compline 9 P.M.

And Sir Gawain replied, "Maiden, with God's help I promise to put all my powers at your service whenever you want: just tell me."

But the knight of the cart did not say he promised her anything in his power: rather, he pledged — like one whom Love made rich, mighty, and bold in all things — that without delay or fear he would promise whatever she desired and put himself entirely at her bidding.

"Then I'll tell you," the damsel said, and did so. "Truly, Sirs, Meleagant, a very strong, big knight, son of the king of Gorre, has taken her into the kingdom whence no foreigner ever returns, but must stay in that country in slavery and exile."

He asked her to continue: "Damsel, where is that land? Where can we find the way there?"

She answered, "Oh, you'll find out. But know that you will meet many hardships and ugly passages: it's not an easy place to get into, except by leave of the king. His name is Bademagu. Actually, one can get in, by two very dangerous routes, really bad entrances. One is called the Water-bridge, because the bridge is under water. There is as much water between the bridge and the bottom as there is flowing over it, no less, no more: the bridge is exactly in the middle. And it's only a foot and a half wide, and the same thick. It's a good dish to refuse — and that's the less dangerous route. Also, between here and there are plenty of adventures I'm not even mentioning.

"The other bridge is worse: so much more dangerous that no one has ever got across it, for it cuts like a sword, so everybody calls it the Sword-bridge. Now I've told you the truth as far as I can."

But he kept questioning her: "Maiden, if you would be so kind, teach us the two roads."

And she answered, "This one is the straight road to the Water-bridge, and that one leads right to the Sword-bridge."

Then the knight, the cart-rider, said, "Sir, I'll share with you ungrudgingly. Choose one of the two roads and call the other mine. Take whichever you prefer."

"My faith," replied lord Gawain, "both crossings are dangerous and hard. Good sense is no help in this choice; I don't know which I'd rather take. But it isn't right for me to shilly-shally when you've said it's my move, so I'll take the Water-bridge."

"Then it's right for me to head for the Sword-bridge without a murmur, and I will."

[700] So the three parted, politely commending each other to God. As the maiden saw them leaving, she reminded them, "Each of you owes me a favor of my choice, whenever I care to ask for it. Be sure you don't forget."

"Indeed we won't, dear friend," answered both knights; and each rode on his own way.

The knight of the cart sank into thought, like a man with no defense against Love's dominion. His meditation deepened until he forgot his very self, and no longer knew whether he was or was not, nor remembered his name, nor knew if he were armed or not, nor whence he came nor whither bound — not a thing did he recall except for one, and for that he had dropped everything else into oblivion. On that one thought he dwelt so that he neither heard, nor saw, nor was conscious of anything else.

His horse bore him rapidly onward; it never took a crooked path, but always the best and straightest. So it happened that he was carried into a field with a ford. On the other side was an armed knight, guarding it, and with him a damsel on a palfrey.

It was already after Nones, but the knight had not grown tired of his thoughts nor quit his brown study. His horse, very thirsty, caught sight of the clear ford and ran toward the water as soon as it saw it.

The knight on the other side cried, "Knight, I guard this ford, and I forbid it you."

Our knight did not even hear him, being still deep in his musings. The horse continued its gallop toward the ford.

The guardian shouted so as to be heard: "Leave the ford, you'd be wise! This is not your crossing!" And he swore his heart out that he would strike the knight of the cart if he rode in.

The latter was thinking so hard he did not hear, and the horse sprang right into the water and left the bank, eagerly beginning to drink.

The knight of the ford said he should pay dearly for it: his shield would not save him, nor the hauberk on his back. He put his horse to the gallop, spurred it to a run, and fell upon him with such a blow that he knocked him sprawling in the middle of the forbidden ford. His spear flew from him and the shield from his neck.

Feeling the water, the knight of the cart started and jumped to his feet, bewildered like a man newly woken. He heard, he saw, he marvelled, wondering who could have struck him. Catching sight of the knight, he cried, "Vassal, why did you hit me, tell me, when I didn't even know you were there and have never wronged you?"

"Yes you have," retorted the other. "Weren't you holding me cheap when I forbade you the ford three times, as loud as I could shout? You must have heard yourself challenged at least two or three times, yet you did step in against my will; and I told you I'd hit you the second I saw you in the water."

Then he of the cart replied, "Curse whoever heard you, or saw you either: I never did. It's perfectly possible — but I was thinking — that you did forbid me the ford. You'll find out it was no luck for you to knock me down, if I could only get your reins in one hand."

"So what? You can hold me by the reins right now, if you dare. I don't care a handful of ashes for your threats or your conceit."

[800] And our knight: "I wish no better. Whatever may come of it, that's what I want to grasp."

So the guardian advanced to the middle of the ford, and the knight of the cart seized his reins in his left hand and his thigh with his right. He pulled, tugged, and gripped him so that his opponent cried out, feeling as if his leg were being pulled from his body. Begging him to let go, he said, "Sir, if you want to fight on even terms with me, get your shield, horse and lance, and joust with me."

"Faith, I won't, because I think you'd run away as soon as I let go."

The other, hearing that, was filled with shame, and replied, "Knight, mount your horse and don't worry; I pledge you truly that I will not run a step. What you said was an insult, and wounds me."

"I've had one promise; now pledge me again that you will not retreat or flee, nor touch me nor attack me till you see me mounted. And I'll have done you a big favor, to let you go after I was holding you."

He had to agree to that; there was nothing else he could do. And when the knight of the cart had his promise, he fetched his shield and spear, which were floating downstream from the ford and had already gone quite a distance. Then he came back for his horse. Having caught it and mounted, he took his shield by the arm-grips and laid his lance in rest, and the two spurred against each other at their horses' best pace.

The defender of the ford attacked his opponent first and struck him so hard his lance broke. The knight of the cart knocked the defender flat into the ford so the water closed over him.

Then he drew back and dismounted, confident of routing a hundred such challengers. From its scabbard he drew his steel sword, and his opponent jumped up and drew his own, bright and good. They fought hand-to-hand, covering themselves with their gold-bright shields. Their swords did good work, never stopping or resting. They had the courage to deal each other heavy blows.

The battle reached a point where the knight of the cart's heart was stung with shame: he thought he could ill afford the path he had chosen if it took him so long to beat one single knight. The day before, if he had met a hundred such in a valley, he would never have believed they could withstand him. He was mortified and indignant to be having such a hard fight, wasting his blows and his time. So he ran at his opponent and harried him until he broke away and left the ford. Leif or loath, he granted our knight the passage.

The knight of the cart chased him until he pitched down on his hands. Then, catching up, he swore by his eyes that he should repent having knocked him into the ford and broken up his meditation.

The maiden whom the knight had been escorting heard these threats. Terrified, she begged him for her sake not to kill him.

Our knight answered that he certainly would: he could have no mercy, for the knight of the ford had insulted him too deeply.

He was advancing on him with drawn sword when the loser

cried out in fear, "For God's sake and mine, have mercy, I beg you!"

[900] "So help me God," he answered, "nobody has ever done me such wrong that if he asks mercy in God's name, I wouldn't pity him at once, for God's sake, as is right. And so I will on you. I shouldn't refuse you, since you have asked me. But first you must promise to surrender yourself my prisoner wherever I may summon you."

The other promised, reluctantly.

The damsel spoke up again: "Sir, by your clemency, since you granted him mercy as soon as he asked you — if you have ever released a prisoner, release this one for me. Let him off his captivity for my sake, on condition that when the occasion comes, I will give you whatever reward you please, as far as I can."

And then he recognized her from her speech,[5] and gave the prisoner free to her. She was embarrassed and pained, thinking he had recognized her, because she had not wanted that.

The knight set off again straightway, the other two commending him to God and asking leave to go their way, which he granted. He rode on.

At Vespers he encountered a maiden, a real beauty, very attractive and well-dressed, who greeted him gracefully and suitably. He answered, "Damsel, God grant you health and good cheer."

"Sir," she said, "my place is ready for you nearby; you'd be well-advised to take it. You may stay there on condition that you lie with me: that is my offer of hospitality."

A good many people would have thanked her five hundred

5. Chrétien explains nothing of this recognition. We are left to conjecture that this maiden may be the same one as at the crossroads, to whom Lancelot and Gawain promised favors (p. ooo).

times for that favor; but he was all downcast and returned quite a different answer. "Maiden, I thank you for your hospitality and I value it. But as for lying with you, if you please, I could very well do without that."

"Without that I won't do a thing for you, by my eyes."

So the knight, unable to do anything else, agreed. His heart was sore at granting her request; if only the promise wounds it, how sad it will be at bedtime! Much pride and much sorrow are in store for the maiden escorting him. Apparently she loved him so much she would not let him off the agreement.

Since he had granted her wish and decision, she led him to a bailey, the most beautiful from here to Thessaly, encircled by high walls and deep water. There was no man inside but the one she was expecting. The damsel had had several beautiful rooms fitted for her quarters, and a generous-sized hall.

Riding along a river, they arrived at this dwelling, whose drawbridge had been let down for them to cross. They entered over it and found the tile-roofed hall open. Passing in the door, they saw a dais covered with a big wide tablecloth, with dishes served forth on it, candles lit in their holders, silver-gilt mugs, and two pitchers, one full of mulberry wine and the other of strong white. Beside the table, at the head of a bench, they found two basins full of hot water for washing their hands, and on the other side, a beautifully worked white towel for wiping them.

No valet, servant nor squire was to be seen in that manor.

[1000] The knight took his shield off his neck, hung it on a hook, and reached his lance up into a rack. Then he jumped down from his horse and the damsel from hers; he was glad she did not wait for his help in dismounting. As soon as she was down, she ran into one of the rooms, fetched him a short scarlet cloak and put it on him.

The hall was far from dark, though the stars were already shining; inside were so many big twisted candles burning that the light was very bright. Having settled the cloak round his neck, she said, "Friend, here are your water and your towel. No one is handing them to you because in this house you'll see no one but me. Wash your hands and sit down when you're ready: the hour and the meal invite you, as you see. Wash, and take your seat."

"Gladly." He sat down, and she next to him, greatly contented. Together they ate and drank until it was time to rise.

As they got up from dinner, the maiden said to the knight, "Sir, go on outside and amuse yourself. No offense — you'll only be out there till you think I'm in bed, please. Don't be annoyed, because then you can come in, if you want to keep your promise."

He answered, "I'll keep your promise and come back when I think it's time." Then he went out and stayed in the courtyard a long time, until he had to go back, for he must needs keep his word.

Arriving back at the hall, he did not find the girl who was making herself his friend: she was not there! Unable to see or find her, he said, "Wherever she may be, I'll hunt until I have her." He did not put off his search, because of his promise to her.

Entering a room, he heard a girl cry out, the very one he was supposed to lie with. Then he caught sight of the door of another room standing open and went to it. Full in view he saw a knight had knocked her over and was holding her crosswise on the bed, all uncovered.

The damsel, feeling certain he would rescue her, shrieked, "Help! Help! Knight, my guest, if you don't get this man off me he will ravish me before your eyes! You're supposed to be lying with me, as you promised; is this man going to force his will on me while you look on? Noble knight, stir yourself, help me, quick!"

Her guest saw that her ravisher was holding her basely stripped to the belly-button; much embarrassed and grieved he was that the man should touch her skin to skin. Not that the knight of the cart desired her nor felt a whit jealous. But the door was guarded by two knights, fully armed, holding naked swords; after them were four servants, each with an axe fit to split a cow down the spine like a broom- or juniper-root.

Our knight stopped in the doorway, thinking, "God, what can I do? Since I'm involved in as big an affair as Queen Guinevere's, [1100] I mustn't be chicken-hearted, being on this quest for her. If Cowardice lends me her heart and I follow her orders, I'll never find what I'm seeking. I am shamed if I stay here. And now I scorn myself for speaking of stopping; it makes my heart dark and sad. Now I'm ashamed, now I'm grieved: I feel like dying for having hesitated so long. May God never have mercy on me if I'm boasting: I'd rather die with honor than live with disgrace.

"If my path were clear, what honor would I win, if these people bowed me through without a challenge? Then, no lie, the worst man alive could pass through. And I hear that poor girl keep crying for my help, reminding me of my promise, and bitterly reproaching me."

So he went up to the door, stuck his head and neck through the window and looked up.[6] He saw the swords coming and dodged back. The knights could not stop the swings they had started; both swords struck the ground and shattered.

6. "Up through the window." One wonders how this door was made. Hardly a doorlet near the bottom through which castle guests put out their sollerets at night to be polished. A Dutch door open at the bottom?

Once the swords were broken, our knight was much less worried about the axes. He jumped in among them and with his elbow struck first one servant, then another. The nearest two he knocked flat with arm and elbow; the third missed him; the fourth attacker struck and slit his cloak and shirt, and broke the white flesh of his shoulder so the blood flowed. But the knight, stopping for nothing nor complaining of his wound, advanced with even longer strides till he grabbed by the temples the man who was raping his hostess. He will be able to keep his promise before he leaves. Willy-nilly he jerked her attacker upright. Meanwhile, the servant who had missed him was coming after him as fast as he could, raising his axe for another blow, planning to split his head to the teeth.

But our knight, knowledgeable in self-defense, held the other knight toward him. The axeman got him where the shoulder joins the neck so they split apart. The knight of the cart quickly took the axe, grabbing it from his hands, and dropped the man he was holding, because he needed to fight: the two knights and three remaining axemen were attacking him fiercely. He nimbly jumped between the bed and the wall and cried, "All right! Have at me! If you were twenty-seven, as long as I've got this niche, you'll have a hard enough fight and won't even tire me."

The damsel, watching him, said, "By my eyes, you'll never need to fight any more where I am." And at once she dismissed the knights and servants. They all left the room without a pause or a murmur. "Sir," she continued, "you have upheld me well against all my household. Now come, I'll lead you." Hand in hand they entered the hall, which did not cheer the knight at all: he would have been quite happy without her.

A bed was made up in the middle of the room, with sheets far from dingy: white, and broad, and fine. Nor was the mattress of straw or hard cushions, either. [1200] It was covered with a pair of silk damasks. The maiden lay down in it, but did did not take off her shift.[7]

The knight took great pains over taking off his shoes and undressing. Anxiety was making him sweat, but in the midst of his anxiety, Promise beat and overcame him. Was he under duress? It amounted to that: he was forced to go lie with the damsel. Promise summoned him to do so.

So he threw himself down, but did not take off his under-tunic, any more than she had. He took great care not to touch her, but kept far away and lay back-to, speaking no word more than a monk who is forbidden to talk in bed [or "monk, who is forbidden to talk, after he (the knight) had stretched out in her bed"]. Nor did he turn his eyes toward her or anywhere else. He could not put on a good face.

Why not? Because it did not come from his heart, which his entire will had directed elsewhere, so he was not at all attracted to what would charm anyone else. The knight had only one heart, and it was no longer his own, but pledged to another, so he could not lend it to still a third. It was fixed in one place by Love, who rules all hearts. All? No, only those she values; and therefore the heart she thinks fit to take under her rule should value itself the more. This knight's heart was highly prized by Love, so she ruled it more strictly than the rest, giving it such pride that I will not blame him for abandoning whatever Love forbade and concentrating on what she wanted.

The damsel could tell perfectly well that he despised her company, would gladly forego it, and would never seek her again, since he was not snuggling up to her. She said, "If you wouldn't mind, Sir, I'll leave and go sleep in my own room,

7. "Did not take off her shift." People usually slept naked.

and you'll be more comfortable. I don't think my company cheers you much — please don't be offended if I tell you my thoughts frankly. Now rest for tonight, for you have fulfilled your promise to me so well that I have no right to ask anything more of you. I'll commend you to God and leave." She rose.

The knight was not at all saddened, but gladly let her go, like a man who was the devoted lover of someone else.

The damsel saw this clearly, went into her own room, went to bed naked, and said to herself, "From the time I first knew a knight, I have never met one except this whom I'd value a farthing. I suspect, I guess that he has in mind something so big that no knight ever dared undertake so dangerous or hard a quest. God grant he achieve it." With that she fell asleep till daylight.

As soon as dawn broke she hastened to rise. The knight also woke, dressed and armed himself without help. The girl entering saw him already dressed and greeted him, "Good day to you."

"The same to you, Damsel," returned the knight, adding that he was impatient to have his horse led out.

She had it brought and said, "Sir, I would go with you a long way on your road, if you dare escort me. You should, according to the usages and customs dating from [1300] before us in the realm of Logres."

Those customs and freedoms were as follows, at that time: if a knight found a damsel or girl alone, no more than he would cut his own throat would he treat her with anything but honor, if he cared for his reputation. Should he rape her, he would be shamed at every court for the rest of his days. But if another knight were escorting her, if she attracted him enough to fight him for her and win her by force of arms, then he could wreak his will on her without incurring shame or blame. That is why the damsel said that if he dared escort her under this custom, nobody could hurt her and she would go with him.

He answered, "No one shall do you any harm, I promise, which he hasn't first done to me."

"Then I'll go with you." She had her palfrey saddled. Her orders were promptly followed: both her palfrey and the knight's horse were led out. The two riders mounted without squires and set off at a great pace.

The damsel talked to the knight, but he paid no attention to her words, refusing instead to answer. Thought pleases him: conversation annoys him. Love kept reopening the wound she had given him, and he never bandaged it, for cure nor for health. He had no desire to seek a poultice nor a doctor, unless his wound got worse; he would even seek this wound!

So they rode as straight as the roads and paths led them, until they sighted a fountain. The fountain was in the middle of a field, with a stone beside it. On this rock some person unknown had forgotten a gilded ivory comb. Never since [the giant] Ysoré's time had any wise man or any fool seen such a beautiful one. In its teeth had stuck a good half-handful of the person's hairs who had been using it.

The damsel, perceiving the fountain and its stone, did not want the knight to see them, so she turned into another path. He, happily feeding on his beloved musings, did not notice at first that she was leading him out of the way. But when he did notice it, he feared he had been deceived, thinking she was turning aside to flee some danger. "Wait, Damsel: you're not going right. Come this way. I don't think anyone ever got on well by leaving this road."

"Sir, we'll go better this way, I'm sure."

"Maiden, I don't know what you're thinking, but you can see this is the straight, beaten track. Since I've set out on it, I won't turn another way. Please come along, because I am taking this path right now."

So they rode until they approached the rock and saw the comb. "Never in my memory have I seen such a beautiful comb as this," observed the knight.

"Give it to me," the girl said.

"Gladly, Damsel." And he bent down and picked it up.

When he had the comb in his hand, he gazed at it for a long time, admiring the hairs. At that the maiden began to smile. Seeing this, he prayed her to tell him why.

She answered, "Hush, I won't tell you a word this year."

"Why not?"

"I don't feel like it."

[1400] Hearing this, he adjured her, like a man who believes a friend should never lie to their friend for any price: "Damsel, if there is anything you love with all your heart, by that I conjure you, beg you and pray you to stop concealing this from me!"

"You plead too weightily. All right, I'll tell you, with no lies: that comb, if ever I knew anything, was the Queen's, I'm sure of it. And you can believe me that those hairs you see, so beautiful, bright and shiny, in its teeth, come from the Queen's head: they never grew in any other meadow."

The knight answered, "Faith, there are plenty of kings and queens. Which do you mean?"

"Upon my word, Sir, King Arthur's wife."

On hearing that, the knight had no strength to keep from keeling over: he had to lean against his front saddle-bow. The maiden seeing him was startled and bewildered, thinking he would fall. She was frightened, and no blame to her, believing he had fainted. And he as good as had, he was very close to it, for he had such a pain in his heart that for quite a while he lost all speech and color. She dismounted and ran as fast as she could to help him and prop him up, for she would not for anything see him fall to the ground.

Seeing her, he felt embarrassed, and asked, "What brings you over to me?"

Never think she told him the real reason, since he would have been ashamed, worried, angered and hurt if he had known the truth. So she took care not to tell it, but replied tactfully, "Sir, I've come to get the comb. I dismounted because I'm so anxious to hold it that I couldn't get it soon enough."

Quite willing for her to have the comb, he gave it to her, drawing out the hairs so gently he did not break one. Never has mortal eye seen anything honored so deeply: he started worshipping them and touched them a hundred thousand times to his eyes, his lips, his forehead, his cheek. There was no joy he did not take in them: he held himself blissful, he held himself rich. He tucked the hairs into his breast, near his heart, between shirt and skin. He would not have traded them for a cartload of emeralds and garnets. He felt that boils or any other sickness could never attack him again. He sneered at pearl-potion, pleurisy-plaster, treacle, and even St. Martin and St. James, for his faith in these hairs was so great he cared for no other help.

But what were the hairs like? You will think me both mad and a liar if I tell the truth. When the fair is full, on the Monday when the most goods are there, the knight would not want the whole thing, it's a proven fact, if he did not find the hairs there. If you insist on the truth: if one looked at gold alongside the hairs, gold purified a hundred thousand times and refined as many more, the gold would have been darker than night compared with the most beautiful day we've had this summer. Why should I make a long story of it?

The damsel quickly remounted, carrying the comb, while the knight rejoiced and took pleasure in the hairs at his breast.

[1500] After the clearing they found a wood and continued in the same direction until the path, narrowing, forced them to ride single file, since there was no way to lead two horses side by side. The girl, ahead of her escort, rode briskly straight ahead. At the narrowest point, they saw a knight approaching.

Even though it was a long way, she recognized him and said, "Sir knight, do you see that man coming toward you, fully armed and ready for battle? He is surely expecting to take me away with him, with no resistance. I know that's what he's thinking, because he loves me and is acting unreasonably. In person and by messengers he's been begging me for ages. But my love is barred to him, because I couldn't love him for anything. With God's help I'll die before I love him in any way. And I know that now he's all pleased and happy as if he already had me home free. But now I'll see what you will do: now it will show, if you're brave. Now I'll see, now it will show, if your protection can save me. If you can, I'll truthfully call you brave and worthy."

He answered, "Go on, go on," which meant, "I don't care — since you're in a panic over nothing — about what you just said to me."

As they rode on talking so, the other knight was not slow in galloping to meet them. He hurried because he had no thought of losing; he considered himself favored in beholding the thing he most loved. As soon as he reached her, he greeted her with heart and mouth and said, "To what I most want, have least joy of, and sorrow most for, welcome wherever she comes from!"

It would not have been right for her to hoard her words so as not to return his greeting, at least with her mouth. And the knight felt very rich that she had saluted him, though it did not pollute her lips nor cost her anything. If he had jousted outstandingly in a tournament that very hour, he would not have been so proud, nor felt he had won such honor and worth.

To make himself even prouder, he took her by the bridle-rein and said, "Now I will take you away. I must have been sailing a straight course today, since I've arrived at such a good port. Now I am comforted for all my misery: from peril I have reached port, from great grief great joy, from great pain great health. Now I have all my desire, when I find you like this and can lead you off with me right now, with no shame."

She answered, "Much good may it do you: this knight is escorting me."

"Well, this must be a poor convoy, because I'm taking you away now. I think this knight will have eaten a peck of salt before he gets you away from me. I don't believe I've ever seen a man I couldn't win you from. And now I find you so handy, even if it grieves him, I'll take you away before his eyes, and let him try his best to stop me."

The other knight, despite the arrogance he heard, did not get angry, but with no boasting simply challenged him: "Sir, take your time, don't waste your words, but speak a little temperately. [1600] Your rights will never be infringed, if you have any. As you know, the girl has come here under my escort. Let go her rein; you've been holding her too long, and she does not even care about you."

Her lover said he would be burnt if he did not take her away willy-nilly.

He of the cart replied, "It wouldn't be right if I let you; in fact, I'd fight first. But if we want to fight, we can't possibly in this path. Let's ride on to an open road, or a meadow or a field."

The other said he asked nothing better and added, "I quite

agree. You're not wrong about this path's being too narrow. My horse will be so cramped by the time I turn him round, I'm afraid he'll break a thigh." Then he turned, painfully but without wounding or damaging his horse, and went on, "Actually, I'm sorry we didn't meet in an open space before other people, for I'd be glad to have them see which of us fought better. But come on, we'll look: near here we'll find a wide open field."

They rode to a meadow where maidens, knights, and ladies were playing various games, since it was a beautiful place. Their games were not mere pastimes, but also chequers and chess; some were enjoying different dice-games and others Twenty Questions. Most were playing these games, and the rest reenacting their childhood with all sorts of dances and singing, tumbling, jumping, and strenuous wrestling.

Across the field sat a middle-aged knight, already white-haired, on a Spanish sorrel with golden harness and saddle. He sat with one hand gracefully on his hip, in his shirt because of the fair weather, watching the games and dancing. A cape all fur and scarlet hung from his shoulders. In another part of the field, along a path, sat as many as twenty-three armed men on good Irish horses.

At the arrival of our trio, everyone stopped their fun and the whole field shouted, "Look, look, here's the knight who was ridden in a cart! Nobody play while he's here! Curse whoever has fun, curse whoever deigns to play while he's around."

Meanwhile the son, the knight who loved the damsel and already considered her his, had ridden up to the white-haired knight and was saying, "Sir, I have great joy. Listen, whoever cares to hear: God has granted me the thing I have most wanted in all my life. Having me crowned king would be a lesser gift, I'd be less grateful and gain less, for this prize is excellent and beautiful."

"But I don't know yet whether it's yours," replied his father.

The son shot back, "Not know? Can't you see? For God's sake, Sir, never doubt it, when you see me holding her. I met her just now riding through this forest where I came from. I believe God was leading her to me, so I've taken her for my own."

"I still don't know whether that man will allow it, whom I see riding after you. He's coming to challenge you for her, I believe."

During this conversation, [1700] the dancing and singing had stopped because of the knight they saw coming. They would have no more fun and games, for spite and displeasure at his presence.

The knight of the cart, without pausing, rode quickly after the maiden. "Unhand the damsel, knight, for you have no right to her. If you dare, I will defend her on the spot against you."

Whereupon the old knight put in, "Didn't I know it? Dear son, don't hang on to the girl, but let her go."

That by no means pleased her lover, who swore he would not surrender her: "God never give me joy if I leave her to him. I've got her and I'll keep her as my own liege property. My shield-strap would be broken and the grips and I'd have no more faith in myself or my armor or my sword or my lance, before I'd turn my dear lady over to him."

His father said, "I won't let you fight, whatever you say. You're foolhardy. Do as I tell you."

The son, in his pride, threw back, "Am I a child to be scared off? I can truly boast that in all the sea's circuit, where there are many knights, there's none so good I would leave her to him, and none I couldn't force to back down in short order."

"Granted, dear son, that's what you think, you're so sure of your strength. But I don't want and shan't want today for you to try yourself against this man."

"I'd be acting shamefully to take your advice. Curses blight whoever follows it and backs down for you, if I don't fight fiercely. It's true I'm only buying family trouble; I could get a better deal elsewhere, because you're trying to trap me. I know that anywhere far away I could win more honor. Nobody who didn't know me would try to change my mind, but you keep nagging and needling me. I'm all the more hurt because you scolded me. You know quite well that whoever reproaches someone's desire, they only burn for it the more. But if I ever quit anything for you, God never give me joy. I'll fight in spite of you."

"My faith to Saint Peter," said his father, "I can see that persuasion doesn't work. Scolding you is a waste of time; but I'll soon build you such a case that you'll have to give in, lief or loath, for you'll be on the losing end."

With that, he called all the knights, who rode up to him, and ordered them to hold his son, whom he could not persuade. "I'll have him tied up before I let him fight. All of you are my men, and owe me faith and friendship. By whatever you hold under my lordship I command you, and also beg you. I believe my son is acting insanely, and if he disobeys me, it comes from his pride."

The men replied that they would hold the young man so no further urge to fight would overtake him, and willy-nilly he would have to give back the girl. Then they all went and seized him by the arms and neck.

"Now, don't you think you've been a fool?" asked his father. "Admit it. Now you have no power to fight or joust, whatever grief it may cost you. Agree to what I want, you'll be wise. [1800] And do you know what my idea is? To ease your sorrow, let's you and me follow that knight, if you want, today and tomorrow, through wood and field, each on his ambling horse. We might soon find him such a man as I'd let you try yourself against and fight to your heart's content."

His son agreed, against his will, perforce. Unable to change the plan, he said that for his father's sake he would do without her, but they both should follow the knight.

When the people in the field saw what was happening, they all said, "Did you see? The knight from the cart has won such honor that he's leading away the beloved of our lord's son, and our lord will follow him. Surely he must believe the knight has some good in him, if he's letting him take her. So a hundred curses on whoever stops their fun any more on his account. Let's go back to playing." And they began again with their games, singing and dancing.

The knight turned at once, not lingering in the field; and the maiden did not lag behind waiting for his escort: off they both went in a hurry. The son and his father followed at a distance. They rode till Nones through a mown field, and in a beautiful site found a monastery with a walled graveyard by its chapel.

It was no base or foolish act for the knight to enter that monastery on foot to pray to God. The damsel held his horse until he returned. When he had finished his prayers and was walking back, a very old monk appeared coming toward him. As they met, he asked him politely what was inside those walls. The monk answered that there was a cemetery, and the knight said, "Take me to it, so God help you."

"Gladly, Sir." And he led him there.

Into the graveyard he took him, among the most beautiful tombs from here to Dombes or on to Pamplona. Each had letters spelling the names of those who would lie within. Our knight began reading them to himself, and found, "Here will lie Gawain, here Louis, and here Yvain." After these three he read many other names of chosen knights, the worthiest and best, both from that country and from others.

Among the tombs he found one of marble, which seemed the

most beautiful work of them all. He called the monk: "These tombs here–what are they for?"

"You've seen the letters and understood them; you know what they say and what the tombs mean."

"Tell me what that biggest one is for."

The hermit [sic] answered, "Oh, I'll tell you. That monument surpasses any other ever made. Not I nor anyone has ever seen one so rich or well-painted. It's beautiful inside and even more outside. But never you mind about that, for it will do you no good: you'll never see the inside of it. If anyone wanted to open this tomb, it would take seven big strong men, for it's covered with a slab. Be sure that to lift it would take seven men stronger than you or me. The letters on it say, "He who raises [1900] this slab by his single strength will free the men and women imprisoned in the land whence neither clerk nor noble returns once he has gone in: never has anyone come back. They hold foreigners captive, but those of the country come and go as they please."

At once the knight went to lay hold of the slab, and he lifted it as if the weight were no trouble, better than ten men could have done with all their might.

The monk seeing this wonder was so astonished he practically fell over; he had never expected to see the like in all his life. "Sir, I would very much like to know your name. Will you tell it me?"

"Not I, on my faith," answered the knight.

"I'm sorry for that. But if you'd tell me, it would be a great courtesy, and you might win much credit. Where are you from?"

"I'm a knight, as you see, born in the realm of Logres. That's all I want to say. And tell me please, who is to lie in this tomb?"

"Sir, the one who will free all those trapped in the kingdom of no escape."

When the monk had told all his tale, the knight commended him to God and all His saints. Then, with nothing further to do, he returned to the damsel. The hoary monk accompanied him out of the church. They reached the middle of the road, and as the maiden was mounting, the monk told her everything the knight had done inside, and begged her to tell him his name, if she knew it.

She admitted that she did not, but dared assure him of one thing: there was no such knight living as far as the four winds blew. Then leaving the monk, she galloped after the knight.

Now the pair following them rode up and found the monk alone in front of the church. The older knight in his shirtsleeves said, "Sir, tell us, have you seen a knight escorting a damsel?"

He answered, "It's no trouble to tell you the whole story; they have just left. And the knight was inside there and performed such a feat that he lifted the slab all by himself without a bit of trouble, right off the big marble tomb. He's on his way to rescue the Queen, no doubt he will rescue her, and all the others too. You know it yourself; you've often read the inscription on the slab. Truly, no knight ever born or horsed has equalled this man."

At that the father said, "Son, what do you think? Isn't he valiant to have done that? Now you know who was wrong, you or me. I would not for all of Amiens have you fight him, but you put up quite an argument before we could prevent you. Now we can go home, for we'd be stupid to follow him farther."

His son answered, "I agree: following won't help us. Let's go back, whenever you please." It was sensible of him to return.

The damsel stuck close to the knight, trying to make him listen to her, [2000] desirous of learning his name. She asked him to tell her, time after time, until in exasperation he said,

"Haven't I told you I'm from King Arthur's realm? Upon my faith to God and His might, you will not find out my name!"

Then she asked his leave to go back, and he was glad to grant it. So the damsel departed and the knight rode on until late alone. Just after Vespers, as he continued on his way, he saw a knight emerging from the woods where he had been hunting. His helm was laced, and the game God had granted him was lashed onto his large iron-grey hunter. This vavasour[8] rode quickly to meet our knight and invited him to stay.

"Sir, it will soon be night. It's time to take shelter, you'd be right to. And I have a house nearby where I'll take you. You've never been better lodged, if I can help it. If you're willing, I'd be delighted."

" And so would I," answered our knight.

The vavasour straightway sent his son ahead to spruce up the house and hurry the cooking. The young man did as he was told with no hesitation, willingly and obediently, and rode briskly off.

The others, in no hurry, followed the same road until they reached the house. The vavasour had as his wife a very well-brought-up lady, and five sons whom he loved dearly: three youths and two knights; and two pretty, well-mannered daughters, still unmarried. They were not native to the country, but imprisoned there, and had been for a long time. They had been born in the kingdom of Logres.

The vavasour led the knight into his courtyard. His wife came running to meet them, and out poured his sons and daughters. Everyone offered their help, greeted him and got him off his horse. The sisters and the five brothers scarcely paid any attention to their lord and father, knowing he preferred

---

8."Vavasour." The lowest rank of feudal nobility, a vassal of a vassal.

them to act so. They honored and welcomed their guest, and when they had disarmed him, one of his host's daughters put her own cape round his neck, taking it off hers.

Whether he was well served at supper I won't discuss. And after the meal, they were not shy of talking about various matters. First the vavasour asked his guest who he was, and from what country; but he did not press him for his name.

He answered promptly, "I am from the realm of Logres, and have never been in this country before."

Hearing that, the vavasour was completely taken aback, and his wife and all his children grieved for their guest and told him, "Alas that you came here, dear Sir, it's ill for you. Now you will be like us, in slavery and exile."

"Why, where are you from?"

"Sir, from your country. In this land are a lot of brave fellow-countrymen of yours in slavery. Curse this custom and the man who maintains it, that no foreigner comes here but is forced to remain: the land keeps them. [2100] Whoever wants to enter can, but then he must stay. Now you're done for too; I don't believe you'll ever get out."

"Oh yes I will, if I can."

And the Vavasour replied, "What? You think you can leave?"

"Yes, please God, and I'll certainly do my best."

"But then all the others could get out free too! Because when one man has got clean away, all the rest will surely be able to go without hindrance." Then he remembered hearing that a knight of great excellence was entering the country in force, for the Queen held captive by Meleagant, the King's son. The vavasour said to himself, "I do believe this must be the man. I'll tell him so." So he said to the knight, "Sir, don't hold back any of your concerns from me. I promise to advise you as best I can. I'll benefit too if you succeed. Tell me the whole story, for your good and mine. I think you have come into this country for the Queen, among this lying people, worse than heathens."

"For nothing else," answered the knight. "I don't know where my Lady is held, but my intention is to rescue her, and I need advice. Tell me, if you know."

"Sir, you've chosen a hard route. The road you're on takes you straight to the Sword-bridge. Believe me — you do need advice — you should go to it by a safer road, and I can give you an escort."

The knight, wishing the shortest path, asked him, "Is it as straight from here as this road?"

"No, it's a longer road but safer."

"Then I don't want it. But advise me about this road, for I'm ready to take it."

"Indeed, Sir, that would be no credit to me. If you go this other way, tomorrow you'll reach a stretch where you could easily get hurt, called Stony Gap. Shall I tell you a little about how bad it is? Only one horse can walk abreast; two men couldn't go side by side. And the passage is heavily guarded. You wouldn't be allowed through when you got there. You'd take many a sword-cut and lance-thrust, and give back some too, before you got through."

When he had described all this, a knight stepped forward, one of his sons, and said, "Father, I will go with this knight, if it doesn't displease you."

At that one of the younger sons got up and said, "I will go too."

Their father readily gave them both leave. Now our knight will not be traveling alone, and he thanked them, very glad of the company. So the conversation ceased and they took the knight to bed, to sleep if he felt like it.

At break of dawn he rose. The two who were to ride with

him saw him and got right up themselves. The knights armed and went to say good-bye. The young son took the lead, and so they rode together until they reached Stony Gap, just at Prime.

[2200] In the middle rose an earthwork with a man on it. As soon as the travelers drew near, this guard saw them and bellowed, "He's come for no good! He's come for no good!"

On the earthwork appeared a mounted knight in fresh armor, flanked by men-at-arms holding sharp axes. As our knight approached the passage, the one watching him rudely taunted him about the cart: "Vassal, you are bold—foolhardy—stupid to enter this country! No man should ever come here who's been in a cart. God never give you joy of your venture!"

They spurred toward each other as fast as their horses could carry them. The guardian of the pass shattered his lance and dropped the two pieces. Our knight hit him in the throat right above the lining of his shield and knocked him down on his back on the stones.

The axemen sprang out, but missed him on purpose, having no desire to hurt him nor his horse. He saw they were not planning to harm him, so without bothering to draw his sword he rode past without hindrance, and his companions after him.

One said to the other that no such knight had ever lived, and none could compare with him. "Wasn't that a wonder he did, forcing his way through there?"

"Dear brother," said the knight, "hurry back to our father and tell him about this adventure."

The young man swore he would not go tell him, nor leave that knight until he had dubbed him a knight too. His brother should go home with the message if he felt so strongly about it.

So all three rode on together until about Nones, when they met a man who asked who they were. "Knights," they answered, "going about our business."

The man said, "Sir, I would like to offer you hospitality, you and your companions." He addressed the knight who looked like the lord of the other two.

He answered, "I couldn't stop for the night at this hour. It's a poor knight who stops and rests at his ease when he's undertaken such a quest. My business is such that it will be a while before I find a lodging."

But the other continued, "My house isn't near here, it's some distance ahead. You can come there, knowing you'll stop at a proper time, for it will be late by the time you get there."

"All right, I'll come."

So they started, the man ahead leading them and the others after him abreast across the road. When they had ridden a good way, they met a squire galloping along on a cart-horse as fat and round as an apple. He cried to the man, "Sir, Sir, hurry! The captives from Logres have massed to attack those of this country, and begun a battle and a fight and a mêlée, and they say a knight has crossed the border who has fought in many places, and they can't stop him, wherever he wants to go, from getting there, whoever objects. [2300] Everyone in the place is saying he will free them and put down our side. Hurry, hurry, I tell you!"

The man set his horse to the gallop, and our travelers (who had overheard) were delighted, eager to help their side. The vavasour's son said, "Sir, hear what that servant says. Let's go help our people, who are fighting those from here."

Their escort was dashing off without waiting for them, headed straight for a fort built on a hill. He ran to the gate, the others spurring after. The bailey was enclosed with a high wall and a ditch. As soon as they got inside, there fell—so they could not get back out—a portcullis at their heels.

They cried, "Come on, let's go, we won't stay here." And they followed their guide, at more than a walk, until they reached the exit, which was not barred to them. But as soon as they were outside, another portcullis fell behind them. They were dismayed, seeing themselves shut in,[9] for they thought they were enchanted.

But our knight (I should tell you more about him) had a ring on his finger whose stone had the virtue that no spell could hold him once he had looked at it. He held the ring before his eyes, gazed at the jewel, and said, "Lady, Lady, so help me God, I now have great need of your help." This lady was a fairy, who had given him the ring and nursed him in his youth.[10] He trusted firmly that wherever he might be, she would help and rescue him.

But he could see, when he had called her and looked at the ring, that here was no enchantment: he could tell they really were shut in. They reached the barred door of a low and narrow postern and all drew their swords and struck until they had chopped through the bar.

Once outside the tower, they saw the fight had started down in the fields, a fierce engagement. There must have been a thousand knights on either side, and at least as many commons. As they rode down to the field, the vavasour's son spoke sensibly: "Sir, before we get there, I think we'd be wise to find out which side our people are on. I don't know which way they're coming from, but I'll go, if you like."

"I do: go ahead, and get back fast."

Fast he goes and fast returns, with "Our luck is in: I've seen that our men are certainly those on this side."

Now the knight advanced to the fray. He met another knight, jousted with him, and struck him so hard in the eye that he

9. "Outside — shut in." The wall must have a gate-tower under which they are caught: they have gone out of the castle courtyard, the portcullis prevents their return, and the postern door is ahead of them.

10. "Fairy." Von Zatzikhoven's *Lanzelet* fills us in on the knight's youth; Chrétien only mentions the fairy patroness and the name "del Lac."

layed him out dead. The younger son dismounted, took the knight's horse and arms and outfitted himself neatly. As soon as he was armored, he mounted and took the shield and lance, long and stiff and painted. At his side he belted the sword, sharp, shiny, and bright, and rode into battle after his brother and his lord. The latter had been holding his own very well in the mêlée, breaking, splitting, and shattering [2400] shields, lances, and hauberks. Neither wood nor iron could save those he attacked; he either crushed them or rolled them dead from their horses. All by himself he was fighting well enough to undo the whole other side. And the two who had come with him were doing all right themselves.

The people of Logres wondered, not knowing him, and whispered enquiries about him to the vavasour's sons. So many kept asking that finally they told them, "Lords, this is the one who is to set us all free from exile and the misery we've been living in this long time. We should do him great honor, since to deliver us from prison he has passed through such dangers, and will pass more yet. He has much to accomplish, and he has accomplished much."

Not a soul but rejoiced when the news reached them. Everyone heard it, everyone learned it. From their joy grew their strength, and they laid on, killing many of the others, hurting them worse for the skill of one knight, I do believe, than for all the rest put together. Had night not been so close, they would all have been routed; but the darkness grew so heavy the combatants had to part.

After the sides had separated, all the captives came clustering round the knight, in anything but a bellicose mood. From every side they took his reins, greeting him: "You are welcome, dear Sir!" And everyone said, "Faith, Sir, you shall stay with me!" "Sir, for God and His name's sake, don't stay anywhere but with me!" What one said, all said, since each was eager to lodge him, young and old alike. They all said, "You'll be more comfortable at my place than anyone else's." Everyone said that about himself, pulling the knight away from each other because each wanted him; they nearly came to blows.

He said their argument was pointless and stupid. "Quit this debate! It's not helping you or me. To quarrel among ourselves does us no good; we should help each other, instead. Fighting isn't the way to get me to stay with you. You should concern yourselves with giving me lodgings which will win you all honor by advancing me on my way."

Everyone burst out again, "That's my place!" "No, mine!"

"You still haven't got it right," said the knight. "I think the wisest of you is a fool, the way I hear you squabbling. You should further my quest, and instead you're trying to turn me aside. If each of you, one by one, had done me all possible honor and service — by all the saints they pray to in Rome, I couldn't be more grateful if I'd received your kindness than I am for the intention. So God grant me thrive, your goodwill cheers me as much as if each of you had already done me great honor and kindness, so let's count the will for the deed."

Thus he out-argued them and calmed them down, and they led him to a rich knight's house along the road. Everyone laid themselves out to serve him. They honored and attended and made much of him all evening until bedtime, for they held him very dear.

In the morning, when it was time to part, each one wanted to go with him and offered himself and pushed forward. [2500] But the knight cared for no other attendance than the two he had brought with him, so he left with them and no more. That day they rode from morning until evening without meeting any adventures.

Riding fast, they emerged from a forest late in the day and at its edge saw a knight's house, with his wife, who looked like a good lady, sitting by the door. Catching sight of them, she stood up beaming and greeted them: "Welcome! I trust you will stay at my house. You've found your lodging: dismount."

"Madam, those being your orders, we will get down and stay at your house tonight."

They dismounted, and the lady had the horses led away, for she kept a lovely household. She called her sons and daughters, who arrived promptly, polite and attractive youths, knights, and pretty girls. Some she told to unsaddle the horses and tend them well. Not one demurred: rather, they did it cheerfully. She had the knights disarmed; her daughters jumped to the job. Once unharnessed, the guests were given two short cloaks to wear. They were soon led into the house, a very handsome one.

But the master was not there: he was in the wood, and two of his sons with him. But soon he returned, and his well-trained household rushed out the door to meet him. They hurried to untie and clean the game he brought and told him, "Sir, Sir, you don't know: you've got two knights for guests!"

"Praise the Lord," he answered.

He and his two sons made much of their guest, and the rest of the household were not backward. They set about doing their best at what was to be done. Some hastened to get the meal served, some to light the candles. These lit and burning, they fetched towels and basins and passed round water for hand-washing, and they were not stingy with it. Then everyone rose and went to their place at table. Nothing burdensome could be seen in that household.

During the first course, a knight arrived outside the door, prouder than a bull (a very proud animal). He was armed cap-apie and sat his horse with one foot in the stirrup and the other thrown in graceful fashion over the horse's mane. There he came without anyone's noticing, until he appeared before them and said, "Which is it, I want to know, so mad, proud, and brainless as to come into this country thinking he can cross the Sword-bridge? He will exhaust himself in vain: his journey is wasted."

Our knight, in no way confounded, answered confidently, "I'm the man who plans to cross that bridge."

"You? You? How dared you think of it? You should have laid plans you could carry out. Remember the cart you rode in. I don't know if you're ashamed of that ride, but nobody in his senses would have ventured on so great a quest [2600]when such disgrace rested on him."

The knight hearing this did not condescend to answer him one word.

But his host and all the rest, naturally, were surprised beyond measure. "Oh, Lord, what a misfortune," said each to himself. "Curse the hour when carts were first conceived and built, for they are vile, hateful things. God, what was he accused of? Why was he ridden in a cart? For what sin, what debt? This will be a reproach to him all his days. If he were clear of the charge, then you couldn't find a knight while the world lasts with proven valor to match this one. Gather them all together and honestly, you wouldn't find so handsome or noble a knight," they all said.

The newcomer arrogantly took the floor again. "Listen, knight, the one going to the Sword-bridge. If you want, you can cross the water lightly and easily. I'll have you rowed over soon enough in a boat. But if I feel like charging you toll, when

I get you on the other side, I'll take your head – or else I won't. It will be up to me."

Our knight replied that he was not looking for ill-fortune. He would not for anything stake his head on that chance.

The other retorted, "If you won't do that, then whoever is shamed or sorry, you shall come out here and fight me man to man."

Our knight teased him: "If I could refuse, I'd be glad to forego it. But I guess I will fight, since I must take a spot of exercise."

Before leaving the table, he told the lads serving him to saddle his horse and fetch his armor, which they hurried to do. Some armed him, others brought his horse. Believe me, as he walked out fully armed, holding his shield, and mounted, he wouldn't be overlooked among the handsome and worthy. The horse seemed so suitable it must be his, and the shield he gripped by the straps; and the helmet laced over his head fitted so well you would never have thought it was borrowed. You would have liked his looks so well, indeed, as to say he was born and had grown that way.

Outside on the jousting-field waited the challenger. As soon as they sighted each other, they spurred together at full speed and force, landing such blows with their lances that both weapons bent, bowed and flew to shivers. With their swords they sliced shields, helms and hauberks; they cut the wood, they burst the iron, until they wounded each other in several places. In their wrath they hacked each other as if on a bet. But often their swords slipped and fell on the horses' croups; they were soaked with blood to the flanks, until both fell dead.

Their mounts fallen, the knights confronted each other on foot. Had they hated each other to the death, [2700] their attacks could not have been more fierce. They rained sword-strokes on each other like a gambler dropping pennies into the pot, never stopping, two and two for every throw. But this was quite a different game: no throw of the dice, but blows, vicious battle, and cruel fighting.

Everyone had come out of the house: lord, lady, daughters, and sons. No man or woman, family or guest was left inside: all were lined up in the broad field watching the fight.

The knight of the cart called himself a coward when he saw his host watching him and noticed all the others staring. A shiver of anger shook his whole body, for he felt he should have beaten his opponent long before. Then he struck him so hard his sword almost reached the other's head. He fell upon him like a storm, advancing on him and forcing him backward, taking ground until the challenger was almost out of breath and had very little fight left in him.

Then our knight recalled that he had basely thrown the cart in his face. By the time he got through with him, not a thong nor strap remained uncut round his neck. Then the knight of the cart knocked the helmet flying from his head, and the ventail down. He drove him until he had to sue for mercy. Like the lark who cannot withstand the hawk, and has no refuge, since he can overtake and outsoar her. So that knight, full of shame, came to beg the other's mercy, since he had no alternative.

When he of the cart heard his prayer for mercy, he neither touched nor struck him, but asked, "You want mercy?"

"Now, that's an intelligent thing to say. A fool should ask. I never wanted anything so badly as I need mercy now."

"Then you'd have to get into a cart. You have no hope in anything you might say to me, if you don't get into a cart, because you have such a fool's mouth as to basely reproach me with it."

The beaten knight answered, "God forbid that I should get into one."

"No? Then you'll die."

"Sir, you can do that, but for God's sake I ask your mercy, on any condition except having to ride in a cart. There's no sentence, no matter how severe, that I wouldn't agree to, except that one. I really think I'd rather be dead than have undergone that disgrace. You couldn't ask me anything else so grievous but I'd do it, for your mercy and grace."

As he was pleading for mercy, there came across the field a maiden ambling on a tawny mule, with her cloak undone and her hair unbound, holding a whip which she was plying on the mule. But in fact, no horse at full gallop ever went so fast but that mule ambled faster.

To the knight of the cart the maiden said, "Sir, God grant your heart perfect joy in whatever delights you most."

He, glad of her greeting, answered, "God bless you, maiden, and give you joy and health."

Then she told him what she wanted: "Sir, I have come to you from far away, with much trouble, to ask a favor [2800] which will deserve as great a reward as I can ever give you — and I think you'll be needing my help sometime."

He answered, "Tell me what you want, and if I have it, it's yours right away, if it's nothing too hard."

"It's the head of this knight you've defeated. And indeed, you never met such a wicked or false one. You'd never be sinning, but rather doing a good work, for he is the untruest thing that ever was or will be."

When the loser heard that she wanted him killed, he said, "Don't believe her, for she hates me. I beg you to have mercy on me by God, Who is Son and Father, and made His mother of one who was His daughter and handmaid."

"Oh, Knight," cried the girl, "don't believe this traitor. May God give you joy and honor as great as you could wish, and grant you success in what you've undertaken."

Our knight was so caught that he stood stock-still, weighing whether to give the head to the maiden who asked him to cut it off, or to cherish this knight so far as to take pity on him. He wanted to grant both his and her request: Generosity and Mercy ordered the granting of both boons, since the knight of the cart was both generous and merciful. But if she got the head, Mercy would be defeated and killed; if she didn't, Generosity would be undone. In such a bind, in such distress Mercy and Generosity held him, each spurring and torturing him. The head deserved to be given to the maid who requested it; but on the other hand, it could command him by his pity and nobility. Having begged his mercy, shall the loser not be granted it? This had never happened to our knight, to refuse any opponent, however hostile, as soon as he was beaten and had to cry mercy. He had never even felt like refusing.

Nor will he deny mercy to this suppliant, since such is his intention. And the maiden who wants the head, shall she have it? Yes, if he can. "Knight," he said, "you must fight me again. I will have so much mercy on you, if you want to protect your head, as to let you get your helmet and give you time to re-arm your body and head as best you can. But know that you shall die if I beat you again."

He answered, "I ask for nothing better and seek no further mercy."

"I'll improve your chance even more by fighting without moving from this spot."

The other armed himself and charged back to the fight like

a madman. But our knight beat him ever faster than before.

At once the maiden cried, "Don't spare him, Knight, whatever he may say. He surely wouldn't spare you if he'd beaten you even once. Listen, if you believe him, he'll trap you again. Cut off his head, good knight; he's the falsest man in the kingdom or the empire — and give it to me. You should, for I can reward you very well some day. And he, [2900] if he can, will entangle you again with his words."

The knight, seeing his death approaching, screamed loudly for mercy, but no cries nor speeches availed him. Our knight seized him by the helmet, slashed all the laces, and knocked the ventail and bright coif of mail off his head. Still he kept crying as loud as he could, "Mercy, for God's sake! Mercy, Vassal!"

"Upon my salvation, I will never have mercy on you, since I've given you a second chance already."

"Oh, you would be sinning to believe my enemy and kill me so."

And the girl, anxious for his death, on the other side adjures him to cut off his head quickly and not believe his words.

He struck. The head flew across the field and the body fell.

The maiden was contented. The knight picked up the head by the hair and handed it to her, who was overjoyed and said, "May your heart have as much joy of the thing it most desires as mine has now of the thing it most hated. Nothing grieved me but his living so long. There is a reward waiting for you from me which will stand you in good stead. This service you have done me will redound to your credit, I promise you. Now I shall go, and I commend you to God: may He guard you from hindrance." She left, and they commended each other to God.

Everyone in the field who had been watching the fight was filled with joy. They hastened to disarm the knight, making merry and honoring him all they knew how. They washed their hands again, eager to sit down to their meal, happier than usual; and they ate very cheerfully.

After a long dinner, the vavasour said to his guest seated beside him, "Sir, we once came here from the realm of Logres. We were born there, and we wish you honor and riches and joy in this country on your quest."

"God hear you," he answered.

When the vavasour had yielded the floor, one of his sons spoke up: "Sir, we should put all our powers in your service, we should give rather than promising. You'd do well to take them; we shouldn't wait till you ask. Sir, never mind about your horse being killed, for in our stable we've got a good strong one. I want you to have that much from us: take our best horse in place of yours. You certainly deserve it."

"I'd be glad to," he replied.

Then they had the beds prepared, and lay down. At dawn they rose promptly, got dressed, then addressed themselves to their journey. As he left, he used all courtesy, saying good-bye to the lady, the lord, and all the others. But I'll tell you, so you won't miss anything, that our knight would not ride the gift horse they gave him at the door. Instead, I want you to know, he made one of his companions mount it while he got on the other's horse; he preferred it so.

Once each was mounted, the three rode off, [3000] with the leave of their host, who had served and honored them the best he could. Straight on they rode until the day was waning, and reached the Sword-bridge toward evening, after Nones.

At the end of this terrible bridge they dismounted and looked at the cruel water, black and loud and swift and deep, ugly and fearful as the devil's river, so dangerous and deep that nothing in the world, once fallen in, but would be swept away as if in the wild sea. The bridge across it was different from all others: the like never was nor ever will be. I tell you truly, there was never so bad a bridge or plank. For over that cold water the bridge was a white-polished sword, but the sword was strong, stiff, and as long as two lances. On each side stood a thick stump, into which the blade was stuck. Nobody need fear falling by its breaking or bending, although it did not look as if it could bear much weight.

The two knights accompanying the third were discouraged, because they thought there were two lions or leopards at the opposite bridge-head, chained to a block of stone. The water, the bridge and the lions threw them into such a fright that they trembled with fear and said, "Sir, believe your eyes; you are forced to. This bridge is wickedly built, wickedly put together. If you don't turn back now, you'll repent it too late. Prudence demands it; there are times like this.

"And suppose you got across — it couldn't happen. You can't hold the winds or stop their blowing, nor tell the birds to stop singing and never dare sing again, nor could a man go back into his mother's womb and be reborn. It would be an impossibility — no more than one could empty the sea. [Even if you were across,] can you imagine that those two raging lions chained there won't kill you, suck the blood from your veins, eat your flesh and then gnaw your bones? I'm brave enough, even daring to look at them steadily. If you don't take care, they'll kill you, be sure. They'll make short work of tearing you limb from limb, knowing no mercy. So now, have pity on yourself and stay with us. You'd be sinning against yourself to knowingly put yourself in such danger of certain death."

With a smile, he answered, "Sirs, many thanks for your concern for me; it comes from your love and good-will. I know you would never want harm to befall me. But I have faith that

God will guard me in all things. I'm no more afraid of this
bridge or this water than of this dry land. I will risk going that
way and crossing it. I'd rather die than turn back."

They did not know what else to say to him, but both wept
and sighed heavily for pity. He prepared himself the best he
knew how for crossing the rapids. But his preparations were
strange: he took the armor off his feet and hands. He won't be
in one piece when he reaches the other side! [3100] He will
get a good grip on the sword, keener than a scythe, with bare
hands, and feet stripped of sollerets, stockings, and ankle-
pieces. Little he cared if he wounded his hands and feet; he
would rather maim himself than fall off the bridge and bathe
in the water he could never escape. Amid great pity he made
his way across, and in great pain, wounding his hands, knees,
and feet. But Love, his guide, soothed and healed him, so he
found his sufferings sweet.

On hands and knees he proceeded as far as the other side.
Then he recalled the two lions he thought he had seen from
across the river, and looked round for them. There was not so
much as a lizard: not one thing to harm him. Raising his hand,
he looked at his ring for a test. Finding neither lion he thought
he had seen, he realized he had been deceived: no living creature
was there.

The men on the other bank, seeing him across the stream,
rejoiced fittingly, unaware of how badly he was hurt. As for
the knight, he counted himself lucky to have taken no more
damage. He dried the blood from his wounds all over his shirt,
and noticed a tower in front of him, so strong he had never
laid eyes on a stronger; it could not have been better.

King Bademagu had leaned out a window: a clever man,
keen for honor and goodness, desirous above all of dealing
honorably in all things. Leaning next to him was his son, who

always did everything in his power to the contrary, for dishonor pleased him: he never tired of committing baseness, villainy, and treachery. From above, the two had watched the knight crossing the bridge with much hardship and pain. Meleagant changed color with wrath and resentment, well aware that he would now be challenged for the Queen. But he was a knight to fear no man, however strong or fierce. Had he not been dishonorable and cruel, there would have been no better knight than Meleagant. But his heart was wood, lacking all sweetness or mercy.

What upset his son rejoiced the king. He knew for certain that the man who had crossed the bridge was better than any other; for no one would have dared cross it who was inhabited by Cowardice, who shames her hosts even more than Valor honors hers. That is why Valor cannot accomplish so much as Cowardice and Sloth. It's true, never doubt it: one can do more ill than good.

I could expatiate on these topics, if it would not delay me. But I will turn back to my story, and you shall hear how King Bademagu schooled his son, saying, "Son, how fortunate that you and I came to this window. We are rewarded with a full view of the bravest deed ever achieved. Tell me, aren't you grateful to the man who has done this feat? Make peace with him and give him back the Queen. You will never win honor in a fight with him—in fact, you could get badly hurt. [3200] So act like a wise and courteous knight, and send her to him before he sees you. Honor him in your land by giving him what he has come to seek, before he asks you, for you know he comes in quest of Queen Guinevere. Don't show yourself stubborn, foolish, or proud. If this knight is alone in your country, you should bear him company; for one brave man should gravitate to another and honor and praise him, not hold aloof from him. He who gives honor, the honor is his. Be sure the honor will be yours if you honor and serve this man, who must be the best knight in the world."

Meleagant answered, "Curse him if there's not one as good or better." He was misjudging himself, to count himself no worse. He continued, "I suppose you're wanting me to fold my hands and feet and swear fealty to him and hold lands from him? So help me God, I *would* become his man before I gave her back. She will never be surrendered by me, but kept and defended against anyone stupid enough to dare come hunting for her."

The King pursued his argument: "Son, you would be courteous to leave your stubbornness. I advise you, I beg you to settle down. For you know it would shame this knight not to win the Queen from you in battle. He would certainly gain more credit taking her as a prize than as a present. I'm sure he isn't looking for her to be handed over peacefully, but expects to fight for her; so you'd be smarter to rob him of his fight. Do keep the peace, I urge you. If you scorn my advice, I shan't care if you get the worst of it, and you could get badly hurt. For this knight has nothing to fear except you: for all my men and me, I grant him truce and surety. I have never been false to my word, a traitor nor a villain, and I'm not about to start, for you nor for a stranger. I don't want to praise him to you, but I promise this knight shall not lack for anything, arms or horse, but he shall have it, since he has shown such bravery in reaching here. He shall be well looked after, and safe from every man but only you. And I remind you that if he can withstand you, he need fear no one else."

"I've heard enough. You'll say what you please," said Meleagant, "and stop when you please, but I don't care what you say. I'm not such a hermit or philanthropist or paragon of chivalry that I'll give him the thing I love most. His business won't be finished so smoothly: things will go quite differently from what you and he are hoping. Even if you help him against me, we won't give in to you. If he and you and all your men have a truce, what do I care? That would never dishearten me: on the contrary, so guard me God, I'd be glad if he had no one to beware of but me. And I'm not asking you to do anything for me which could be called falseness or treachery. You be as much of an upright king as you want, and let me be vicious."

"What, you won't behave otherwise?"

"No," said Meleagant.

"Then I'll say no more. Do your best, because I'm leaving you and going to speak to that knight. [3300] I will offer him my help and advice in all matters and put myself entirely at his disposal." So the King went down and had his horse saddled. They brought him a great charger, which he mounted with the stirrup, and took some of his people with him: three knights and two attendants, no more.

They rode downhill toward the bridge until they saw the knight wiping off the blood and bandaging his wounds. The King expected to have him as a guest for a long time while the wounds healed, but he might as well have expected to dry up the sea. Bademagu made haste to dismount, and the badly wounded knight stood up to greet him, showing no more trace of the pain in his hands and feet than if he had been completely whole.

The King saw the effort he was making [or: that he was losing strength?], ran to greet him, and said, "Sir, you astonish me by reaching us in this country. But be welcome, for no one has ever attempted this, no one ever has or ever will be so brave as to venture himself in such danger. Be sure I love you all the more for accomplishing what no one has dared to think, let alone do. You will find me kind, courteous, and honorable. I am the king of this country, and my counsel and service are all yours. I believe I know what you are in quest of, I think you are seeking the Queen."

"Sire, you think right: nothing else brings me here."

"Friend," the King told him, "there will be difficulties before you get her. And you are badly wounded; I can see the cuts and the blood. You won't find the man who brought her here so friendly as to give her to you without a fight. But you must stay and have your wounds tended until they are well healed. I'd give you the three Marys' own ointment,[11] or even better, if it could be found, for I am eager for your comfort and your cure.

"The Queen has a good prison, and no one lays a finger on her, not even my son, much as he rues it, the man who brought her here: no one has ever raged as he does. I am very well-disposed toward you, and so God save me, I'll be glad to give you whatever you need. My son shall never have such good armor — no matter how angry he is with me — that I won't give you equally good, and a suitable horse. And I will be your surety among all men, whoever objects. You're never to fear anyone but the man who brought the Queen here. Nobody ever threatened another the way I did him, and I nearly banished him from my kingdom, I was so angry, because he wouldn't give her back to you — and he my own son. But don't you worry: unless he bests you in fair fight, I'll never let him do you a pea's worth of harm."

"Thank you, Sir," said the knight. "But I'm wasting too much time here, which I don't want to lose. I'm not suffering for anything, and I haven't any wounds which bother me. Just

11. "Three Marys' ointment." What the three women brought to anoint Christ's body.

take me where I can find him; with the arms I have on me I am ready now to give blows or take them."

"Friend, you'd better wait two weeks or three [3400] until your cuts are healed. A rest of at least a fortnight would do you good. I could never allow, never watch you fight in such arms or in such a state."

He answered, "If you would permit it, there would never be arms I'd rather fight in than these, and not a second's delay, putting-off, or waiting. But for you I'll do this much: I'll wait until tomorrow. And God help anyone who suggests my waiting longer."

Then the King agreed to his will and had him led to his lodgings, urgently ordering his escort to spare no pains in serving him; they obeyed.

King Bademagu, desirous of keeping the peace if he could, returned to his son and spoke like a peace-maker. "Dear son, do reach an agreement with this knight without fighting. He has not come here for sport, bow-hunting nor the chase: he's come on a quest and to increase his honor. And he badly needs a rest, from what I've seen of him. Had he taken my advice, this month or next he wouldn't have been spoiling for a fight — but he is. If you give him the Queen, are you afraid you'll be dishonored? Don't worry: no reproach can come to you. On the contrary, it's a sin to keep something one has no right to. He actually would have loved to fight here and now, and he without a hand or foot whole, but all cut up."

"You're upset over foolishness," Meleagant told his father. "On my faith to Saint Peter, I won't take your word in this affair. May I be drawn by horses if I believe you. If he wants his honor, so do I mine; if he wants his good reputation, so do I mine; and if he's wishful to fight, so am I more, a hundred times."

"I see you're looking for trouble," retorted the King, "and you'll find it. Tomorrow you shall try your strength against this knight, if you're willing."

"May I never be hampered by pity for him! I'd rather it were today than tomorrow. Just watch if I act any tamer than usual. Now my eyes are darkened, now I look downcast. Until I fight I'll never find relief or happiness, and nothing that happens can please me."

The King could hear that neither advice nor entreaty was doing any good at all, so reluctantly he left Meleagant. Taking a fine strong horse and good armor, he sent them to the man they would benefit. And there was an old man, an excellent Christian, none truer in the world, who knew more about curing wounds than the whole University of Monpelier. That night he did all he could for the knight, as the King had ordered him.

The news spread to all the knights, maidens, ladies, and lords of all the country round, and they came long journeys through the entire district, natives and foreigners, riding fast all night until dawn. What with both parties, there was such a press in front of the tower at daybreak that [3500] one could not stir a foot.

The King got up early, feeling distressed about the battle, and approached his son again, who already had his helmet (made in Poitiers) laced on. There was no possibility of postponement nor reconciliation; the King asked very nicely, but could achieve nothing.

Before the tower, in the middle of the square where all the people had gathered, the combat will be held, at the King's command. Soon he summoned the stranger knight, who was escorted into the square full of citizens of Logres. They had assembled the way people flock to the monastery at each year's feasts, Pentecost or Christmas, to hear the organ. For three days all the virgins of King Arthur's realm had been fasting, going barefoot in rags, that God might grant strength against his opponent to the knight who was to fight for the captives.

Those of Gorre, on their part, were praying for their lord, that God might give him the victory and honor of the battle.

Early in the morning, before Prime had rung, both had been brought to the square, fully armed, on two iron-sheathed horses. Meleagant looked very well and very elegant, nicely fitted in arms, legs, and feet; and his helmet and the shield hung round his neck became him too beautifully. But everyone sided with the other (except those who wished his shame) and declared Meleagant could not hold a candle to him.

When both were in the middle of the square, the King came and halted them, in an effort to make peace, but he could not get his son to agree. So he said, "Rein in your horses at least until I'm up in the tower. It's not too much to ask you to put off your fight till then."

Much perturbed, he left them and went straight to where he knew the Queen was. The night before, she had asked him to put her where she could get a clear view of the combat, and he had granted her request. Now he went to fetch her, glad to put himself out for her service and honor. He met her at a window and stayed at her right hand, reclining at the next embrasure. Quite a lot of other people gathered with the two, knights and prudent ladies and maidens native to Gorre, and many of the captives, deep in their orisons. All those prisoners were praying for their lord, for their hope of rescue lay in God and him.

Without further delay the combatants had the crowd cleared back, nudged their shields into position, and gripped the handles. They spurred so that at two fathoms their lances hit the

middle of each other's shields, burst, and shattered to smith-
ereens. And the horses at full tilt charged into each other,
forehead to forehead, chest to chest. The men's shields crashed
together, and their helms, with a concussion like heavy thun-
der. Not a breast-strap, girth, [3600] stirrup-leather, rein, nor
bridle-strap remained to be broken. The saddle-bows, strong
as they were, shattered. No shame if both men fell to the
ground, since all their equipment had failed.

Soon they jumped up and came at each other straight, more
fiercely than two boars. Taking no time for threats, they dealt
each other great blows with their steel swords, like two men
who hated each other intensely. Often they slashed each other's
helm or hauberk so violently that blood spurted after the iron.
Both fought well, stunning and damaging each other with hard
and ugly blows.

Evenly matched, they fought many rounds, fierce, violent,
and long; one could not tell which to judge better or worse.
But it was impossible for the knight who had crossed the
Sword-bridge not to be weakened by the wounds in his
hands. The people were dismayed — those on his side — to see
his blows fall more feebly. They feared he would get the worst
of it.

They had concluded that he would indeed be defeated, and
Meleagant win, and were talking of it all round. But up in the
tower window was a very bright girl; it occurred to her that
the knight had not set up this fight for her, nor the rest of the
petty folk in the square; he would not have undertaken it but
for the Queen. The maiden guessed that if he knew she was at
the window, in sight of him, watching him, he would recover
his strength and courage. Had she known his name, she would
have liked to tell him to look round a little.

Approaching the Queen, she said, "Madam, for God's honor

and yours and ours, I beg you to tell me — so as to help him — the name of that knight, if you know it."

The Queen answered, "Maiden, I can see nothing wrong in your request, but only good. That knight, I know, is named Lancelot of the Lake."

"Heavens! Doesn't that cheer my heart and make it laugh," said the girl. Springing forward, she shouted to him so loudly that all the people could hear, "Lancelot! Turn round and see who's watching you!"

When Lancelot heard his name called, he wasted no time in turning round. And looking up, he saw the thing in all the world which he most desired to see, sitting at the tower window.

From the moment he saw her, he did not take his eyes off her nor turn his head, but parried behind his back. Meleagant dogged his heels as closely as he could, pleased at the thought that Lancelot had no defense left. The natives were happy, and the captives so grieved they could not stand up, but quite a few sank in a faint to their knees or flat to the ground. Thus there was much joy and sorrow.

Again the maiden called from the window, "Oh, Lancelot, how can you be so foolish as to stop? You always possessed all good and all valor; I don't believe God ever made a knight who could measure up to your worth, and [3700] now we see you in such difficulties! Circle round, so you'll be on the other side facing the tower, since it's so good to look at."

Lancelot was embarrassed and pained to the point of despising himself, when he realized that for some time he had been getting the worst of the fight, and everyone knew it. He jumped back, circled round, and forced Meleagant between himself and the tower. Meleagant strove to turn the fight round again; and Lancelot ran at him and hit him on the shield with all his weight, when he tried to manoeuvre out of position, so hard he staggered twice or more, much to his chagrin.

Lancelot's strength and courage were growing, because Love helped him, and also because he had never hated anything so much as his opponent. Love and mortal Hatred, greater than had ever been before, made him so fierce that Meleagant stopped taking him lightly and became afraid. He had never met so stout a knight, nor had any ever hurt him so badly as this one. Meleagant was glad to keep his distance; he retreated, he yielded ground, fearing and avoiding his blows. Lancelot, not with feints but with blows, drove him toward the tower where the Queen was reclining, whom he had often served and praised. Then he got Meleagant so close that he had to step back, or else he could not see her if he advanced one step. So Lancelot kept moving Meleagant back and forth, wherever he wanted, and kept stopping before his lady, the Queen. Gazing at her had set him on fire, and that ardent flame enabled him to chase Meleagant wherever he pleased. In spite of himself, Lancelot drives him about like a blind man or a cripple.

The King saw his son so overwhelmed he was not even defending himself. Grieved, he took pity on Meleagant; if he could, he would call a halt. But if he wanted to do it properly, he must ask the Queen, so he addressed her: "Lady, I have stood your friend, honored and served you since you have been in my jurisdiction. If your honor was involved, I've been glad to do anything. Now repay me in kind: but the favor I want to ask is one you should not grant me unless from friendship. I can see for certain that my son is getting the worst of the fight. I'm not asking you because I'm sorry for him, but only so Lancelot won't kill him, which he could do. And you don't have to be willing because Meleagant has acted fairly by you and him — he hasn't — but for my sake, by your mercy. Please,

I beg you, tell him to stop hitting him. Thus you could repay my service, if you thought good."

"My dear Sir, at your request, I am willing," replied the Queen. "Even if I hated your son to the death—and my feelings toward him are not friendly—still, you have served me so well that if it pleases you, I'm willing that Lancelot should stop."

She said this in no small voice; Lancelot and Meleagant heard the words.

[3800]A true lover is completely obedient and prompt to do what pleases his beloved. So Lancelot had to obey, who loved more than Pyramus; no one could love more deeply. He heard what she said. No sooner had the last word fallen from her lips — "If you want him to stop, I'm willing" — than Lancelot would not for anything have stirred, nor touched Meleagant, though he had killed him. He did not move, he did not strike; and Meleagant laid on as hard as he could, beside himself with shame and anger at being reduced to have mercy asked on his behalf.

The King, to restrain him, descended from the tower onto the field and said to his son, "What? Is that any way to behave, him not touching you and you hitting him? You're too bloodthirsty, you're valorous out of season! And we KNOW he was beating you."

Meleagant, quite unhinged with shame, retorted, "You've got to be blind! I know you can't see anything. Anyone is blind who says I wasn't beating him."

"Find someone to believe that," said the King. "All these people know if you're telling the truth or lying. We know how it really was." He told his lords to hold his son back, and they hastened to obey, dragging him from the field. But to remove Lancelot did not need great force, since he was anxious to have the fight stopped before he hit him. Bademagu said to his son,

"So help me God, now you must make peace and give him back the Queen. You must drop the whole quarrel and consider it settled."

"Now, that is a useless remark! I hear you talking about NOTHING! Get out! Let us fight and don't butt in!"

The King said he would, "for I know this man would kill you if we let you fight."

"He'd kill me? No, I'd kill him in no time, and beat him, if you'd only let us fight and not interrupt."

The King answered, "So help me, whatever you say will do you no good."

"Why not?"

"Because I don't wish it. I will not give credence to your folly and arrogance, to get you killed. He is insane who wishes his own death, as you're doing without knowing it. I know you hate me for trying to save you. God grant that I may never have to witness your death: it would grieve me too much."

So he spoke and so he lectured him until peace and accord were reached. The terms were that Meleagant should give back the Queen, on condition that Lancelot, one year from the day when Meleagant should summon him, should punctually fight with him again. This condition caused Lancelot no difficulty. Everybody hurried to the peace-making. They arranged that the rematch should be at the court of Arthur, Lord of Brittany and Cornwall. And the Queen must agree and Lancelot pledge that if he failed to appear, she should return with Meleagant and no one should detain her. The Queen and Lancelot agreed to the terms, and so the combatants were reconciled, then parted and disarmed.

It was the custom of the country [3900] that since one captive was leaving, all the others got out too. They all blessed Lancelot, and you may be certain that great joy was called for and felt. Those of Logres assembled to celebrate Lancelot and cried so he could hear, "Sir, indeed, you made us happy as soon as we heard your name. Right away we knew we'd be free." The celebration became crowded, with everyone striving and straining to touch him. The nearer they could get, the more inexpressibly happy they were. Joy and wrath were both present, for the freed prisoners were all given up to joy; but Meleagant and his people had no cause for good feeling and were broody, defeated, and depressed.

The King left the field, not leaving Lancelot behind but taking him along. Lancelot asked to be led to the Queen. "I won't delay you [It's not my decision?]," said Bademagu; "good idea. I'll bring you to Kay the Seneschal, too, if you'd like."

Lancelot in his delight almost fell at his feet.

Bademagu took him directly to the room where the Queen had gone to await him. When she saw the King leading him by the hand, she stood up to greet Bademagu, and acted like a lady offended, casting down her eyes and not saying a word.

"Lady, here is Lancelot to see you; that should really please you."

"Me? Sir, he cannot please me. I have nothing to do with seeing him."

"Heavens, Lady," exclaimed the courteous Bademagu, "where did you get that mood? Surely you scorn the man too much who has served you to the point of often putting his very life in jeopardy on the journey, and has rescued you from my son Meleagant, who has tried you sorely."

"Indeed, Sir, he has wasted his time. I shall never pretend I am in the least grateful to him."

Lancelot stood filled with sadness. But he answered politely like a true courtly lover, "Lady, indeed, that grieves me, and I dare not ask why."

He would have explained himself at length, if the Queen would have listened; but to complete his discomfiture, she would not answer him a word, but withdrew into a private room. Lancelot escorted her to the door with eyes and heart, but his eyes had only a short trip, as the room was too near. They would have loved to go in with her, had it been possible. The heart, a greater and more puissant lord, followed the Queen from the hall, and the eyes were left outside, full of tears, with the rest of his body.

The King remarked *sotto voce*, "Lancelot, I can't imagine what this means or why, that the Queen won't see or speak to you. If ever she would converse with you at all, she shouldn't stand off now, nor deny you a word, considering what you've done for her. Tell me, if you know, for what reason or what crime she treated you so."

"Sir, at this point I wasn't expecting it either. But she doesn't feel like seeing me or hearing what I say. It hurts me."

"Indeed, she's wrong," said the King, "for you risked your very death for her. [4000] Anyway, come on, my dear friend, and we'll go talk to the Seneschal."

"I'd like that," he answered.

Together they went to Kay. When Lancelot reached him the Seneschal's first words were, "How you've disgraced me!"

"I have? How? Tell me," begged Lancelot, "what shame have I done you?"

"A great one: you achieved the feat I couldn't and did what I couldn't do."

King Bademagu left them together and went from the room alone. Lancelot asked Kay if he had been badly hurt.

"Yes, and I still am: I've never been worse hurt than right

now. I'd have been dead long ago, but for the king who's just left. He, in his mercy, has shown me so much kindness and friendship that never — if he knew it — did I lack for anything but it was brought me as soon as he found out. But against the good he's done me there's Meleagant, his son, full of wickedness. In his treachery he called the doctors and told them to dress my wounds with ointments which would kill me! So I had both a father and a stepfather: the king kept having good medicine put on my wounds, wanting to help me be cured quickly; and his traitor son kept having it taken off (because he wanted to kill me) and the bad salve put on. But I know the king knew nothing about that. He would never permit any such foul murder.

"But you don't know about his generosity to my Lady: no border-fortress since Noah built the Ark has been so well-guarded but Bademagu has kept her better, for he won't let his son see her — which galls Meleagant plenty — except before everybody or before the King's own eyes. This gracious king in his mercy treats her, and has from the first, with all the honor she could wish. No one ever wished like her, when she wished things so. And the King esteemed her all the more, seeing her so true.

"But is it true, what they say, that she's so angry at you that in front of everyone she denied you one word?"

"You've heard the truth," admitted Lancelot. "But in God's name, could you tell me why she hates me?"

Kay answered that he did not know, in fact was perplexed.

"Well, let it be as she commands," sighed Lancelot, who had no choice, adding, "I must take my leave now and go in search of Lord Gawain. He has come into this country, and we agreed that he should go straight to the Water-bridge."

Leaving Kay's room, he came before the King and asked

leave for his journey. Bademagu was glad to grant it. But the prisoners whom Lancelot had set free asked him what they should do.

"Everyone who wants may come with me, and those who want to stay by the Queen, do so: it wouldn't be right for them to come with me."

All who wanted rode off with Lancelot, happier than they had been. With the Queen stayed maidens, rejoicing, and many ladies and knights. [4100]But not one of those who stayed wouldn't have been gladder to return to their own country. However the Queen kept them there until Sir Gawain should come, saying she would not move until she had news of him.

The tidings were repeated everywhere: the Queen was free, and all the other captives too, and they could indeed leave whenever they pleased. One would ask his neighbor the details; there was no other topic whenever the people gathered. They were far from sorry the dangerous passages were destroyed, so anyone could come and go: that wasn't how things used to be.

When the natives of Gorre who had not been at the battle found out what Lancelot had done, they assembled where they knew he would pass; they thought the King would be pleased if they seized Lancelot and brought him to him. The knight's party were all unarmed, and therefore were taken by surprise by the attack of the armed natives. No wonder if they captured Lancelot, he being unarmed. As a prisoner they led him back, feet tied under his horse.

Lancelot's people told them, "Gentlemen, you are doing wrong, for the King has granted us safe-conduct: we're all under his protection."

The ambush-party replied, "We don't know about that, but as we've caught you, you'll have to come to court."

Rumor, always quick to fly and run, came to the King that

his subjects had taken Lancelot and killed him. When Bademagu heard that, he was much distressed, and swore on more than his head that the murderers should die: never could they escape, and if he could catch them there would be nothing but hanging, burning, or drowning. And if they tried to deny it, he would never believe them, for they had stricken his heart with too much grief, and shamed him, too. He would be an object of reproach if he did not take vengeance; but he would exact it, no fear.

This same Rumor, traveling everywhere, was repeated to the Queen as she sat at her meal. She nearly killed herself when she heard the news about Lancelot — it was false, but she thought it was true, and grieved so much she could hardly speak. But for the sake of the bystanders she uttered, "Indeed, I am sorry for his death, and rightly, since he came into this country for me, so I am right to mourn him." Then to herself she added, so quietly that no one could hear, that she would never ask for food or drink again, if indeed the man were dead for whose life she lived.

Rising in sorrow from the table, she lamented inaudibly. She was so eager to kill herself that several times she gripped her own throat. But first she made her confession alone: she repented and told over her sins, bitterly reproaching herself and heaping herself with guilt for the sin she had committed against the one she knew had always been hers, and still would be, were he alive.

She grieved so over her cruelty that she lost much of her beauty: repentance for her vicious attack faded and shadowed her complexion, as did her fasting and waking. She rolled all her sins together and brooded over them. As they recurred to her mind, she often sighed, "Alas! What was I thinking of, when my Dear appeared before me, not to welcome him [4200] or even listen to him. When I denied him a look or a word, wasn't I insane? Insane? No, God help me, I was cruel. And I thought I was joking,[12] but that's not the way he took it, and he's never forgiven me. Nobody but me gave him his death-wound, I know it. When he came to me smiling, thinking I would welcome him joyfully, and I saw him but would not see him, wasn't that his mortal blow? When I would not speak to him, I do believe I cut out his heart and his life too. Those blows finished him, I think, and no other troops. Oh, God, can I be forgiven for this murder, this sin? No! The rivers will run dry and the sea perish first.

"Alas, how happy I would have been, how consoled, if once before he died I had held him in my arms. How? Why, both of us naked, for our greater comfort.

"If he is dead, I am wrong not to kill myself. Shouldn't my life be a burden to me, if I survive him, with no pleasure except the pain I feel for him? If that is my pleasure after his death, certainly in his lifetime the pain would have been sweet which I desire now. It's a wicked lady who prefers suicide to suffering for her beloved. But indeed, I shall find great pleasure in a long mourning for him. I would rather live and bear the blows than die and be at rest."

The Queen grieved so that for two days she neither ate nor drank, until they thought she was dead.

There is always someone to carry news, the bad faster than the good. The rumor came to Lancelot that his lady and beloved was dead. Never doubt his distress: everyone could see

12."I thought I was joking." This line explains Guinevere's cold reception of Lancelot (see pp. 65f) better than her purported explanation on p. 75. In a turmoil of feelings which she is not free to acknowledge — passion for Lancelot, anger with Bademagu — Guinevere took hasty refuge in the pose of the Absolute Lady, and inadvertantly, clumsily, hurt Lancelot. She continues the pose on p. 75 because she cannot bear to admit her clumsiness.

he was upset and grieved. Indeed, he was so sad, if you want to know, that he despised his own life and was on the point of killing himself; but first he made a lament. He knotted one end of his belt into a noose, and weeping said to himself, "Oh, Death! How you have entrapped me, making of my very health a sickness. I am sick, yet I feel no pain but the sorrow descending on my heart, and that pain is grievous, even mortal. I only hope it will be: God willing, I shall die of it. What, can't I die unless God wills it? I will, if He only lets me tighten this belt round my neck; that way I think I can force Death's hand and kill myself in spite of her. Death, who never wants anyone but those who don't want her, won't come to me. But my belt will lead her captive, and when I have her in my power, she shall do my bidding. Even so, she'll come too slowly, I am so anxious to seize her."

Then he delayed no longer, but slipped the loop over his head and round his neck. Intent on harming himself, he tied the other end of the belt tightly round his saddle-bow, unnoticed by anyone. Then he let himself slide toward the ground, planning to be dragged by his horse until he died. He scorned to live another hour.

When the people riding with him saw him fallen to the ground, they thought he had blacked out, for nobody noticed the belt he had tied round his neck. [4300] They hastened to pick him up in their arms and set him upright and then they found the belt which, enemy to himself, he had put round his throat. Swiftly they cut it; but it had squeezed his throat so hard that for quite a while he could not speak. All the veins of his neck and throat were nearly burst. Now, even if he wanted to, he could no longer do himself any harm.

It pained him to be guarded; he was on fire with sorrow, still longing to kill himself if nobody were watching. Unable to hurt himself, he said in his mind, "Oh, base vile Death! Death, for God's sake, why had you not the same strength as when you killed my Lady? I suppose you had done that so well you disdained the next job! It was wicked of you to desert me, and will never be counted otherwise. Oh, what service! What kindness! Haven't you set her up beautifully! Curse whoever thanks you for that service. I don't know which hates me worse, Life who desires me, or Death who refuses to kill me. Between them, both murder me.

"But, God help me, it's right that I should unwillingly remain alive. For I should have killed myself as soon as my Lady the Queen showed hostility to me. She did not do that without a reason: there was some good cause, only I don't know what it was. But if I had known, before her soul went to God I would have made it up to her as richly as she wanted, if only she'd had pity on me.

"God, what could my sin have been? I do believe she'd found out I rode in the cart! I don't know what she could reproach me with if not that. That betrayed me. If she hates me for that, God, why was that a crime to harm me? Anyone who could blame me for that never knew Love, for one could never call blameworthy any deed inspired by Love; rather, whatsoever one may do for one's Darling is love and courtesy.

"But I didn't do it for my 'Darling' — alas, I don't know what I'm saying. I don't know whether to call her Darling or not. I daren't put that name to her. But I think I know enough of love to be sure she could not hold me base for that, if she loved me, but call me a true lover; because for her sake it seemed to me an honor to do whatever Love commanded, even get into the cart. She ought to count that as love — indeed, it was the acid test: that is how Love tries her men and knows them. But this service did not seem good to my Lady, as I have found out from her behavior to me. Yet her lover did something for which many people have reproached him, for her sake. I've played a game they blame me for, and made my sweetness my bitterness, for indeed that's the way of people who know nothing of Love, but raise honor to shame. But he who grinds honor into shame does not raise it, but soils it. Well, those who despise Love's subjects are ignorant themselves; they set themselves above her, not fearing her commandments. Surely the man improves who does as Love orders him; everything is allowed, and he has failed if he dares not do it."

Thus Lancelot lamented, and his escort guarding him was doleful.

[4400]But on their way, news reached them that the Queen was not dead. Immediately Lancelot cheered up, and if his previous mourning for her death had been great and strong and violent, his joy at her life was a hundred thousand times greater.

When they came within six or seven leagues of where King Bademagu was staying, he was told news of Lancelot which delighted him: the knight was alive, and coming, safe and well. It was well done on the King's part to go and report this to Guinevere.

She answered, "Dear Sir, since you tell me, I believe it. Had he been dead, I promise you I should never have been happy again. I'd be robbed of all joy if a knight had taken his death in my service."

The King left her impatient for her joy and her dear to arrive. She had no more desire to quarrel with him about anything. But Rumor, who never rests but runs all day every day, came again to her, that Lancelot would have killed himself for her had he been allowed. She was pleased and easily believed it, but for nothing in the world would she have had him much harmed.

Meanwhile, Lancelot arrived at top speed. As soon as the King saw him, he ran to kiss and embrace him. He felt like flying, his joy made him so light. But the joy was cut short by those who had captured and bound him. The King told them it was their evil hour when they came: they were all lost and dead. And they answered that they thought the King had wanted it.

"Me it displeases, but you it suits," he retorted; "and it has done him no harm. You have not shamed him a bit, but only me, who had assured him of safe-conduct. However it happened, the shame is mine. But you will never escape to boast of it."

Hearing the King's anger, Lancelot strove his utmost to bring peace, and succeeded. Then Bademagu led him to see the Queen.

This time she did not cast down her eyes: she went gladly to greet him, showed him all the honor she could, and seated him next to her. Then they could talk to their hearts' content about whatever they pleased—and they did not find themselves short of material, for Love furnished them with plenty.

Seeing himself well-situated, his every word a delight to the Queen, Lancelot said in a low voice, "Lady, I wonder very much why you treated me as you did day before yesterday, when you saw me but never said a word. You nearly killed me with that, but I hadn't the courage to ask you then as I'm asking now. Lady, now I am ready to amend it, as soon as you've told me the sin. I've been much grieved over it."

She replied, "Why, weren't you ashamed of the cart and afraid to get in? You were very reluctant, hesitating for two steps. But I won't scold you for that."

"Next time, God keep me from such a sin. And may He never have mercy on me if you weren't absolutely right. Lady, for God's sake, receive atonement from me now, and if you will ever pardon me, in His name let me know."

"Friend, be completely absolved," she told him. [4500] "I am glad to pardon you."

"Lady, I thank you. But here I can't tell you everything I want to. If it were possible, I would like to converse with you at more leisure."

And the Queen pointed out a window — with her eye, not with her finger — and said, "Come talk to me tonight at that window, when everyone in the house is sleeping. You can come through the orchard. You won't be able to enter nor find lodging: I shall be inside and you outside, because you can't get in. Nor could I come out to you — only my hand or my mouth. But if you want, I will be at the window until tomorrow, for love of you. We can't come together, because in my room between me and the door lies Kay the Seneschal, still sick with his wounds all over. And the door is not left open, but tight shut and well guarded. When you come, take care that no one spies you or discovers you."

"Lady, as far as I can manage it, no spy shall see me, to think or report ill of us."

So they conversed and parted cheerfully. Lancelot left the room so happy he did not remember a single one of his troubles. But he found the night very slow in coming; by the feelings he endured, that day lasted longer than a hundred, or even a year. If only dark had fallen, he would gladly have gone to his rendezvous.

He struggled to defeat the daylight until black night had covered him and wrapped him in her cape. When he saw dusk falling, he pretended to be tired out, saying he had been awake a long time and needed rest. You can well understand, you who have done the same, that his show of being tired and going to bed was for the people of his suite. He was not so enamored of his bed as to stay in it for anything; he couldn't, he wouldn't dare, he wouldn't even want to dare or be able to.

Swiftly and softly he rose, not sorry that no moon or star was shining, and indoors no candle, lamp, nor burning lantern. So he made his way, taking care nobody noticed him. They thought he was asleep in his bed all night. Alone, with no escort, he hurried toward the orchard, meeting no one. He was lucky that a piece of the orchard wall had recently fallen. Through the crack he slipped, and reached the window, where he waited in silence, without a cough or sneeze, until the Queen arrived, in a very white shift. She had not put on any tunic or over-dress, but wore a short cloak over her shift, of scarlet and marmot-fur.

When Lancelot saw the Queen lean into the window-bay, which was barred with thick iron bars, he greeted her most sweetly and she him, as he longed for her and she for him. Their conversation was neither base nor boring. They drew near each other and joined hand in hand. That they could not come together distressed them both immeasurably, and they reproached the bars.

But Lancelot claimed that if the Queen pleased, he would come in with her: the bars would not keep him out.

[4600]She answered, "Don't you see the bars are too stiff to bend and too strong to break? You'd never be able to twist, pull, or loosen them to get them out."

"Lady, don't worry! I don't think iron works: nothing but you can prevent my coming to you. Granted your leave, my path is clear; but if you do not wish, then it's so blocked I could never get through."

"Indeed," she said, "I am willing. My wish does not hold you back. But you must wait until I'm back in bed. And don't make a sound by accident; it would be no joke if our noise woke the Seneschal sleeping here. So I'd better go back, since he'd think no good if he saw me standing here."

"Lady, go back if you want, but never worry about my making a sound. I can pull out these bars so gently I won't strain myself nor wake anybody."

Then she went back, and he set about dismantling the window. He gripped the bars and dragged and pulled until he had them all bent and out of their sockets. But the iron was so sharp that he gashed the first knuckle of his little finger to the sinew, and the next finger also. Yet he did not feel the wounds at all, nor the dripping blood; his mind was elsewhere.

The window was not low, but Lancelot slipped through it nimbly. He found Kay asleep in his bed, and then he reached the Queen's. He worships it and bows down, for he has no such faith in any relic.

She held out her arms to him and embraced him, hugging him close to her breast and drawing him into bed beside her. She gave him as fair a welcome as she could, for it came from her heart and from Love. From Love came her welcome; and if her love for him was great, his for her was a hundred thousand times greater: Love was lacking in all hearts compared to his. In his heart Love revived, and was so totally there that it languished in all others.

Now Lancelot had all he desired, when the Queen welcomed

his company and his comfort, when he held her in his arms and she him in hers. Their play was so sweet to them, with kissing and touching, that in fact a joy and a wonder befell them such as has never been heard or told. But I will continue to keep it silent, for it does not belong in a story. Of all joys the choicest and most delightful is that which the story conceals from us.

All that night Lancelot had much joy and sport. But the arrival of morning distressed him, when he had to rise from his love's side. Getting up truly martyred him, the parting was so painful, he was tortured. His heart pulled to the side where the Queen remained; he could not drag it back, for he was so delighted with her that he had no desire to leave her. His body walked away, but his heart stayed.

He went straight to the window. But so much of his blood remained, bled from his fingers, [4700] that the sheets were stained and spotted. As he left he was grieving, full of sighs and tears. They had made no arrangement for meeting again, which saddened him, but it could not be. Reluctantly he climbed out the window where he had been so glad to come in. His maimed fingers were far from healed. Once out, he straightened the bars and set them back in their sockets, so that from neither front nor back could one tell that any of them had been taken out or bent. As he left, he bowed to the room, behaving exactly as if he were before an altar.

Then sadly he went away, without meeting anyone to recognize him, back to his own room. He got into bed naked without waking anyone. And at Prime he was surprised to find his fingers cut, but it did not worry him, for he realized he had hurt them pulling the window-bars out of the wall. He did not mind: he would rather have had both his arms dragged from their sockets than miss passing through that window. Had he incurred such ugly wounds anywhere else, he would have resented them.

Meleagant, having dressed, approached the room where the Queen lay. He found her awake, and saw the sheets spotted with fresh blood. He nudged his companions and like a man noticing something wrong looked toward Kay's bed, where he also saw sheets stained with blood; for in fact during the night the Seneschal's wounds had reopened.

"Madam!" exclaimed Meleagant, "Now I've found the signs I was looking for. How true it is that the labor of guarding a woman is mere folly and wasted effort. He who guards her the hardest loses her faster than he who doesn't bother. [My father]'s been guarding you from me, all right, but this night Kay has looked on you in spite of him, and had his will of you, as will be proven!"

"How?" asked the Queen.

"I've found blood on your sheets to witness it, since you insist on being told. That's how I know, that's how I prove it: on your sheets and his, I see the blood from his wounds. These are true clues."

Then for the first time the Queen saw the bloody sheets on both beds, and was astonished. Turning crimson with embarrassment, she said, "So God guard me, this blood on my sheets was never brought by Kay. I must have had a nosebleed overnight. I'm sure it came from my nose." And she thought she was telling the truth.

"By my head," said Meleagant, "anything you say is nothing. There's no need to lie: you're accused and indicted and the truth will be proved." Then "Sirs," he said to the guards present, "don't move. See that the sheets are not taken off the bed until I get back. I want the King to support me when he has seen this."

He looked for Bademagu until he found him, fell at his feet and cried, "Sire, come and see something you weren't expecting. [4800] Come see the Queen, and you'll see something incredible which I've found. But before you go, I pray you not to deny me justice. You know what danger I've put myself in for the Queen, and you've been my enemy for it, and you've had her guarded from me. This morning I went to greet her at her levée, and I saw enough to tell me that Kay is lying with her every night. Sir, for God's sake don't mind if I grieve and lament, for it hurts me that she hates and despises me, and Kay lies with her every night!"

"Hush," said the King; "I don't believe it."

"Then, Sire, come and see the sheets, and the state Kay left them in. If you won't take my word, but think I'm lying to you, I'll show you the sheets and bolster bloody from Kay's wounds."

"Well, let's go," answered the King. "I'm willing to look. My eyes will teach me the truth of the matter." He went straight to the room where the Queen was holding her levée. Seeing the bloody sheets on both her bed and Kay's, he said, "Lady, things are bad, if what my son tells me is true."

She replied, "So help me God, never—unless in a nightmare—has such a wicked lie been uttered. I believe Kay the Seneschal is so courteous and honorable as never to occasion reproach; and I don't peddle my body at fairs or deliver it. Kay is never the man to ask such an outrage of me, and I have never been inclined to do it, nor shall I be."

"Sire," said Meleagant to his father, "I shall be very grateful to you if Kay pays for his crime in a manner humiliating to the Queen. It is your place to judge the case, and I beg your justice. Kay has betrayed his lord, King Arthur, who so trusted him as to give her into his care, the thing he most loves in this world."

"Your Majesty, allow me to answer," broke in Kay, "and I will clear myself. May God, when I leave this world, never pardon my soul if I have ever lain with my Lady. I would prefer to be dead than commit so foul a wrong against my Lord. May God never grant me better health than I have now, may death take me this minute if I ever even thought of it. But I know this much about my wounds: last night they did bleed a lot, and got my sheets bloody. That's why your son believes ill of me, but indeed, he has no right to."

Meleagant answered, "So help me God, the fiends have betrayed you. Last night you were too hot, you overstrained yourself, and that must be why your wounds burst open. Nothing you say to the contrary will help you. The blood in both beds proves it: we can see it, it's obvious. A man so proven guilty deserves to be punished. A knight of your standing never committed such a shameful act. You are disgraced."

"Sire, Sire," cried Kay to the King, "I will defend my Lady and myself against your son's charge. He's burdening me with reproaches, but wrongly, wrongly!"

"You can't fight," Bademagu told him; "you're too badly hurt."

"My Lord, if you will permit it, sick as I am I'll fight him, and prove myself innocent [4900] of his accusations."

Guinevere, in secret, had sent for Lancelot. So she told the King she would have a champion to defend the Seneschal against Meleagant's charge, if he dared. And the Prince answered promptly, "There's no knight of yours I wouldn't fight until one of us was beaten, even if it were a giant."

Thereupon Lancelot came in. The room was crowded with knights. As soon as he arrived, in the hearing of all, young and old, the Queen recounted the matter: "Lancelot, Meleagant has charged me with this shame; he has made everyone who hears him believe ill of me, unless you can make him take it back. Last night, he says, Kay lay with me. Because he saw blood-spots on my sheets and Kay's, he says he'll be found guilty unless he can defend himself or someone else will undertake the combat to help him."

"You need never beg when I'm round," returned Lancelot. "God forbid that anyone should believe such ill of you or Kay. I'm ready to maintain in battle that he never even thought of it, if my defense is worth anything. I will champion him to the best of my power and accept the trial by combat."

Meleagant leaped forward, crying, "So God save me, I'm willing, I'm glad of it! Nobody think I mind!"

Lancelot said, "My Lord King, I know about cases and laws, pleas and judgments. A combat over such a charge must not take place without an oath."

Without a moment's hesitation, Meleagant snapped back, "There'll be oaths, all right. Bring the relics here and now: I know I'm right."

And Lancelot retorted, "Never, so help me God, has Kay the Seneschal known such a crime as he is accused of."

At once they ordered the armor brought and their horses led out. The equipment was brought, the combatants armed themselves, their squires finished the arming, and they were ready.

The relics too were brought out. Meleagant stepped forward,

and Lancelot beside him. Both knelt. The Prince, holding out his hand to the relics, swore straight out: "So help me God and the saints, Kay the Seneschal was with the Queen last night in her bed and took all his pleasure of her."

"I take that up as a false oath," replied Lancelot, "and swear on my part that he neither lay with her nor touched her. May God, if He please, take vengeance on the one who has lied, and show the truth. And I will swear another oath, in spite of anyone: if I am granted the victory over Meleagant today, so help me God and these relics here, I will never have mercy on him."

The King was not at all happy to hear that oath.

The oaths sworn, their horses were brought forward, fine ones in all points. Each knight mounted his and sped toward the other as fast as the horse could carry him. At the top speed of their horses the knights struck each other, so that there was nothing left of their lances between the points and their fists. They bore each other to the ground, but neither acted discouraged: up they sprang, [5000] to do each other all the damage they could with the edges of their naked swords. The sparks flared from their helms up to the clouds. They attacked each other with such wrath, their bare swords cutting here and slashing there, meeting and striking each other, that they sought no chance to rest or draw breath.

Bademagu, much distressed, called the Queen, who had gone up to watch from the window-bay in the tower. He called to her for God the Creator's sake to let the combatants be parted.

"Whatever you please," she said. "In good faith, it will never hurt me."

Lancelot clearly heard her answer to the King's request and stopped trying to fight; he withheld his strokes. Meleagant, desiring no rest, hailed blows on him. Throwing himself between them, Bademagu held back his son, who swore he wanted no truce: "I want to fight! I care for no peace!"

His father answered, "Be quiet and trust me, you'll be wise. No shame or harm will come to you if you take my advice: do what's right. Don't you remember you've engaged to fight him at King Arthur's court? And don't you realize it would be much more honor to you there than anywhere else?" He said this in hopes of discouraging Meleagant so he could calm him down and part them.

Lancelot, increasingly impatient to find Lord Gawain, came to take leave of the King and the Queen. With their permission he set out for the Water-bridge under the current, followed by a large crowd of knights. Quite a few were going whom he would have been glad to leave behind. They passed their days pleasantly on their way to the Water-bridge, but were still a league off.

Before they came in sight of it, a dwarf came riding toward them on a large hunter, holding a cat-o'-nine-tails to urge on the beast and to threaten. He asked, as he had been ordered, "Which of you is Lancelot? Don't hide, I'm on your side; speak out, I'm asking for your advantage."

Lancelot spoke for himself: "I am the man you ask for."

"Oh, Lancelot, brave knight, leave these people, do, and come with me alone; I will bring you to an excellent place. Let no one follow us even with their eyes, but just wait here, for we'll be right back."

Lancelot, suspecting nothing wrong, made his whole company stay and followed the dwarf — who had betrayed him. Those awaiting him there had a long time to wait, for the ones who had captured him had no intention of sending him back. He did not come, he did not return, and his companions mourned so deeply they did not know what to do. Everyone said the dwarf had tricked them, and if they were grieved, it would be stupid to ask. Sadly they began searching, but had no idea where to find him or even which way to hunt. So they all took counsel, and the wisest agreed, I believe, as follows: they should go on to the Water-bridge, which was nearby, [5100] and search for Lancelot afterwards with the help of Lord Gawain, if they could find him in wood or field. Everyone agreed to stick to this plan.

They approached the Water-bridge and as soon as they reached it they saw Sir Gawain, fallen off the bridge into the deep water. Now on the surface, now submerged, now they saw him, now they lost him. They came closer and grappled him with branches, sticks, and hooks. He had nothing but the hauberk on his back and the helm on his head, which was worth ten others, and his iron sollerets on his feet, rusted with his sweat; for he had undergone many trials, passed through many dangers and won many battles. His lance, shield, and horse were on the other bank.

Those who pulled him from the water did not think he would live, he had so much inside him. Until he got rid of it, they did not hear a word out of him. But once his heart and pipes were clear and he regained the power of speech, so they could hear and understand him, as soon as he could talk, he did: at once he asked those by him if they knew any news of the Queen. They answered that she was keeping close to King Bademagu, who served and honored her faithfully.

"Has no one else come to this country looking for her?" asked Sir Gawain.

"Yes! Lancelot du Lac, who crossed the Sword-bridge. He has rescued her, and all the rest of us with her. But a dwarf has betrayed him: a hunchbacked, ugly dwarf has played us a dirty trick and lured Lancelot away from us. We don't know what harm he has done him."

"When?" Gawain asked.

"Sir, today the dwarf did that to us, right close to here, when we were coming for you."

"What has he been doing since he came to this country?"

So they told him by turns, not leaving out a word. About the Queen, they told him she was waiting for him; indeed, she would not leave the country until she saw him and heard his news.

But Lord Gawain replied, "When we get away from this bridge, shan't we go hunt for Lancelot?"

There was not a soul who did not advise going first to the Queen; then she could get Bademagu to order a search. For they were sure his son had treacherously had Lancelot imprisoned: Meleagant, who hated him. But wherever he might be, if the King knew it, he would have him set free; so they need not seek him now [or: they could count on that?].

Everyone agreeing to that suggestion, they approached the court where Guinevere and the King were. Everyone assembled there, including Kay the Seneschal, and also the traitor, full and overflowing with treachery, whose capture of Lancelot had dismayed the arriving party. They reckoned he was dead and betrayed, and mourned deeply in their grief.

That was no courteous Rumor which brought this sorrow to the Queen. Nevertheless, she behaved as gracefully as she could. For Lord Gawain's sake it behooved her to rejoice, and she did. All the same, she could not entirely conceal her sorrow. Both joy and grief befitted her: her heart was sore for Lancelot, [5200] but toward Lord Gawain she showed a most cheerful face. No one, hearing the news, but was upset over the loss of Lancelot.

The King was happy at Gawain's arrival and glad to meet him. But for Lancelot betrayed he was prostrated with sorrow. The Queen called upon him to have Lancelot sought up hill and down dale throughout his land, without delay. Lord Gawain, Kay, and everyone else joined in her prayer.

"Leave it to me," answered Bademagu, "and speak no further of it, for I am already persuaded; even without being asked I would order this search." Everyone bowed to him.

Then he dispatched messengers throughout his kingdom, well-known and well-conducted retainers, who asked news of Lancelot all over the countryside. Everywhere they asked, but nowhere could they learn the truth. Not finding him, they returned to where the knights were, Gawain and Kay and all the rest, who said they would go themselves in quest of him, fully-armed, lance in rest, and not send other people.

One day, after their meal, they were in the hall putting on their armor: it was time. They were all ready to ride out, when a serving-youth came in and walked through them until he reached the Queen, who was not looking rosy; she was grieving so for Lancelot, not knowing what had become of him, that her color was faded. The youth greeted her and the King beside her, and all the others, Kay and Lord Gawain. He was holding a letter, which he handed to Bademagu. Suspecting nothing, the King had it read aloud in all their hearing.

The reader could tell them clearly what he saw written on the parchment: Lancelot saluted the King as his good lord, thanked him for the honor and service he had done him, and put himself entirely at his service. Know [said the letter,] that Lancelot was with King Arthur, well and strong. He sent word to the Queen that she should return, and the same orders for Lord Gawain and Kay. And with the letter were plausible tokens, so they believed it. Much they rejoiced: the whole court buzzed with happiness. They declared their intention of leaving the next day as soon as it was light.

As dawn broke they dressed and equipped themselves, mounted and rode away. The King escorted them cheerfully a long way. He led them out of his domains, and as he let them out, he said good-bye to the Queen and all the rest. At their leave-taking, she politely thanked him for doing her such service. With both arms round his neck, she pledged him her service and her lord's; she could promise nothing greater. Sir Gawain did likewise, parting from a lord and friend, and Kay too, and everyone promised the same.

Then they took their road, the King commending them to God. And to all the rest after those three he said farewell, and then turned back. [5300] The Queen did not pause a day for a whole week, nor the group she was leading, until the news reached the court — which delighted King Arthur — that she was approaching; and his heart was also gladdened for his nephew, for he thought that by Gawain's valor the Queen had returned, and Kay, and the lesser folk. The facts were otherwise.

The whole city poured out to meet them, and everyone, knight or commoner, cried as they met, "Welcome, Lord Gawain, who has brought back the Queen and many captive ladies, and given us back the prisoners!"

Gawain answered, "Sirs, you are praising me for nothing. Stop it: none of it belongs to me. Your honor shames me, for I did not arrive in time; by my delay I failed. But Lancelot got there in time, and he deserves such honor as never a knight has won before."

"Then where is he, dear Sir, for we don't see him here?"

"Where?" asked Sir Gawain quickly. "He's at our Lord the King's court, isn't he?"

"No, faith, nor have we heard any news of him in all this country since our Lady was taken."

And then Lord Gawain realized that the letter had been forged, had deceived them: they had been tricked and betrayed by the letter. Then their grief came back on them. Mourning, they reached the court, and the King at once asked for a report. Quite a few people could tell him what Lancelot had accomplished: how by him the Queen and all the captives were freed, how and by what treachery the dwarf took him from them.

This distressed the King deeply, but his heart rose with his joy over the Queen until the joy ended the sorrow. Having what he most cared for, he took little account of the rest.

While the Queen was out of the country, I think the remaining young lords and ladies took counsel among themselves, not knowing what to do. They wanted to get married soon. The decision of the council was to hold a tournament: Lady Poore-Lyttel challenged those of Pomelegoi. The poor performers, they said, they would not speak to, but the best fighters they would love. They published the news and had it cried all through the neighboring lands and the distant ones too; long beforehand they had the date of the tournament announced, to draw more people. And the Queen came back before the chosen date.

When the ladies knew she had arrived, most of them headed straight for the court. Coming before the King, they begged a boon of him. He promised, before finding out what they wanted, to do it.[13] Then they told him they wanted him to let the Queen come watch their tournament. Unable to deny them, he said it was all right by him if she were willing.

The ladies, delighted, hurried to the Queen with, [5400] "Madam, don't take from us what the King has granted!"

13. "Promised, before finding out what they wanted." Not again, Arthur! This rash boon (benign, as it turns out) sets the second half of the romance going as the boon to Kay did the first half.   Modern readers are sometimes bothered by many medieval works' coming in two. If one considers Lancelot and Guinevere's night of love the high point, that leaves a couple of thousand lines of padding. Kelly says, rather, that Lancelot has a dual mission: (1) rescue Guinevere, (2) avenge her and Logres on Meleagant. Each goal is achieved at the end of one section of the poem, both sections being parallel in their incidents. In each,

Arthur grants a rash boon $\begin{cases} \text{to Kay} \\ \text{to the maidens} \end{cases}$

in consequence, Guinevere goes somewhere $\begin{cases} \text{Gorre} \\ \text{Noauz (Poore-Lytell)} \end{cases}$

Lancelot overcomes obstacles to reach her $\begin{cases} \text{many adventures} \\ \text{seneschal's wife} \end{cases}$

Lancelot fights in ways which show his love $\begin{cases} \text{Meleagant (three stages)} \\ \text{tournament (two days)} \end{cases}$

Lancelot is captured $\begin{cases} \text{Gorre people} \\ \text{tower} \end{cases}$

Lancelot is comforted by a woman $\begin{cases} \text{Guinevere} \\ \text{Meleagant's sister} \end{cases}$

Lancelot triumphs $\begin{cases} \text{makes love to Guinevere and she may leave Gorre} \\ \text{kills Meleagant.} \end{cases}$

Also in both sections, though not at the same point in each,

Lancelot receives woe and weal from Guinevere $\begin{cases} \text{cold welcome / night of love} \\ \text{au noauz / au mialz (Poore-} \\ \text{Lytell / the best).} \end{cases}$

"What is it?" she asked. "Don't keep it from me."

"If you want to come to our tournament, he'll never stop you or say no."

And she said she would come, since he gave her leave.

The ladies hastened to send word throughout the kingdom that they would have the Queen with them on the day announced for the tournament. Rumor flew far and near, hither and yon, and spread even to the kingdom whence none used to return. Nowadays, whoever wanted could enter or leave without hindrance.

The news was told and passed on until it reached the house of a seneschal of the dishonorable Meleagant (hellfire burn the traitor!). This seneschal was guarding Lancelot, quartered in his house as a prisoner by his enemy Meleagant, who hated him with a passion.

Lancelot heard the tourney announced, and its date. His eyes were not dry nor his heart cheerful at the news. The lady of the house noticed his depression and took him to task in private. "Sir, for God and your soul, tell me why you are so changed. You aren't eating or drinking, and I don't see you playing or smiling. You can safely tell me what's troubling your mind."

"Oh, Lady, for God's sake don't be surprised if I'm sorrowful. I don't know what to do, unable to be where all the good in the world will be: at the tournament where everybody seems to be going. But if you pleased, if God made you so generous as to let me go, you could be sure I would have the self-control to come back to your prison."

"Indeed," said the lady, "I'd be glad to do it if only I didn't see my death and destruction! But I'm so much afraid of my Lord, that base Meleagant, that I wouldn't dare, because he'd destroy my husband in no time. No wonder I'm afraid of him; you know how vicious he is."

"Madam, if you fear I won't come straight back to your prison after the tournament, I can swear you an oath I'd never break that nothing could keep me from returning right afterwards."

"All right, I'll agree, on one condition."

"What condition, Lady?"

"This," she answered: "that you swear to return, and also pledge me that I shall have your love."

"Madam, all the love I have I will surely give you when I return."

"You think you're fooling me," said the lady laughing. "I know for a fact that the love I asked you for is devoted to someone else. But I'll take what I can get of it and not be choosy. I'll stick to what I can demand, and take your oath that you will bring yourself back to my prison."

Lancelot, as she required, swore by the Holy Church that he would surely return. She thereupon lent him her husband's armor, red, [5500] and a horse he had, wonderfully strong, beautiful, and brave.

He mounted and rode off, armed with excellent gear, fresh and new; and traveled until he reached the Poore-Lyttel lands. He joined their side and took lodging outside the village. No man of worth was ever so housed, for it was little and low; but he did not want to stay in a place where he would be recognized.

In the castle, many excellent knights were assembled, but even more outside. On account of the Queen, so many had come that a fifth could not have been lodged within: for one there were seven, and never a one would have been there except for Queen Guinevere. The barons had set up quarters for five leagues round, in pavillions, shelters, and tents. Also present were an amazing number of noble ladies and maidens.

Lancelot had set his shield at the door of his cabin. For a rest, he had taken off his armor and lain down on a bed which he did not think much of, it being narrow, and the bolster covered with a coarse hempen sheet. Lancelot, all unarmed, was reclining there. As he lay in such poor estate, there came by a boy, a herald, in his shirt-sleeves. In a tavern he had gambled away his gown and his shoes too, and was hurrying along barefoot, coatless, in the wind. He saw the shield outside the door and stared at it, but he could not recognize it nor tell whose it was nor who was to bear it.

Seeing the cabin door open, he went in, and saw Lancelot lying in the bed. When he laid eyes on him, he recognized him, and crossed himself at the sight. Lancelot gave him a look and forbade him to mention him, wherever he might go. If the herald should say he knew him, it would be better for him to have his eyes torn out or his neck broken.

"Sir, I have always admired you, I still do, and in all my life I will never for any money do anything you might resent." And he dashed from the house and made off, yelling, "Here's the man will take their measure! Here's the man will take their measure!"

Everywhere the lad went shouting like that, and people came flocking, asking what he was hollering. He was not so rash as to tell them, but just went on shouting. That was the origin of the expression "take their measure;" our teacher was that herald, for he first used the phrase.

The crowds assembled, the Queen and all the ladies, knights, and others. Left and right were many attendants. At the tourneying-ground was a large timber grandstand, since the Queen was there and the ladies and maidens; never was seen such a beautiful one, so large or so well-made.

The next day, following the Queen, everyone repaired there who wanted to see the fight and who would do better or worse. The knights came by ten and ten, twenty and twenty, thirty and thirty, here four score and there ninety, here a hundred and there more and elsewhere twice as many. The crowd grew so great in front of the grandstand and round it that the tournament was begun. The armed and the unarmed gathered; the lances resembled a great forest: [5600] those who would use them had brought so many that one could see nothing but lances, with their pennants and gonfalons.

The jousters moved off to their jousting, easily finding partners who had come for the same; others limbered up for other knightly exercises. The fields were so full, and the plowland and the clearings, that one could not guess the number of knights, so many were there. But there was no Lancelot at that first assembly. But when he came riding across the field and the herald saw him, he could not help crying, "Look, there's the man will take their measure! There's the man will take their measure!"

They asked him, "Who is he?" But the herald would not tell them.

When Lancelot reached the tournament, he was worth twenty of their best, and began fighting so well no one could take their eyes off him, wherever he rode. On the Pomelegoi side was a valiant and worthy knight, on a horse as swift and light as a moorland deer. This was the king of Ireland's son, an excellent fighter; but everyone was four times as pleased with the knight they did not know. They were all in a fever, demanding, "Who is that fighting so well?"

The Queen drew aside a discreet and sensible maid and said,

"Damsel, you must take a message, and quickly; it's not long. Go down from the grandstand to that knight with the red shield. Say to him in private, 'poor little,' and tell him it's a message from me."

Promptly and properly she did as the Queen asked: followed the knight until she got near him, and discreetly said to him, so no one nearby overheard, "Sir, my Lady the Queen sends you a message by me: I'm to tell you, 'poor little.'"

Hearing the message, he said he would gladly obey, like a knight entirely devoted to her. Thereupon he rode against another knight as fast as his horse could carry him, and missed him when he should have hit him. From then until evening, he never fought except as badly as he could, to please the Queen. And the knight he was charging did not miss, but hit him a great blow with a heavy follow-through, and Lancelot fled. For the rest of the day he did not turn his horse's head toward any other knight. For death itself he would do nothing except what would shame, harm, and dishonor him; he showed fear of everyone who came by.

The other knights, who had esteemed him, laughed at and mocked him. The herald, who had been saying, "This knight will mow them down in swaths!" was downcast and embarrassed, hearing the teasing and jokes of the others: "Now shut your mouth, friend, this guy won't be taking anyone's measure. He's measured till he's broken his yardstick, though we used to admire it."

Most of them said, "What's all this? He was so brave just now, and now he's such a cowardly thing he won't stop to meet any knight. Maybe he did so well at the beginning because he'd never fought before, and when he came he was so strong that no knight, however experienced, could withstand him because he struck like a madman. And now he's learned enough of arms that he'll never want to bear them again in all his life. His heart can't take any more: there's no sadder specimen in the world."

[5700] The Queen was by no means displeased, in fact she was delighted; for now she knew — but did not tell — that this was indeed Lancelot. So all evening until nightfall he made himself out a coward. But Vespers broke up the tournament. As they parted, there was a great argument over who had fought the best. The prince of Ireland thought there was no gainsaying that he had won all the praise; but he was grossly mistaken, for there were several as good. Only the red knight pleased the ladies and maidens, the noblest and the most beautiful: all day they had devoured him with their eyes like no other. For they had seen how well he had fought at first, how brave he was — and then turned so spiritless that he dared meet no knight, but the worst could knock him down and capture him at will.

All the ladies and gentlemen agreed to return to the tournament the next day, and those who won that day should marry the maidens. So they decided and so it was prepared, and then they went back to their lodgings. When they got there, in many places people started talking. "Where's that worst knight, that nothing, that disgrace? Where did he go? Where's he hiding? Where's he gone? Where can we find him? We'll probably never see him again, for Cowardice has driven him away. He has embraced her yoke until there's nothing in the world so shameful. And he's right, for a coward has it a hundred thousand times easier than a brave warrior. Cowardice is an easy mistress, that's why he's given her the kiss of peace and holds all he has from her. Surely Valor would never demean herself to be in him or even sit near him. But Cowardice has cuddled right down into him: she finds him a host who loves her and serves her so that for her honor he's losing his own." So they made fun of him all night, choking in their eagerness to bring out their ill-natured remarks. But often those who speak ill of others are worse than those they blame and scorn.

Everyone said what they pleased, and when day broke they all armed again and headed for the tourney. The Queen was back in the grandstand, and the ladies and maidens, and quite a few knights with them who weren't bearing arms because they were captives or had taken the cross. They stood explaining to the ladies the arms of the knights they most respected.

"Do you see the one with gules a bend or? That's Governau de Roberdic. And see the one after him with an eagle and a dragon side by side on his shield? That's the son of the King of Aragon, come to this country to win praise and honor. Next to him, the knight jousting so well, with the shield parti vert and azure,[14] and on the vert a leopard: that's Ignaure the longed-for, the agreeable, the true lover. And him with the pheasants painted beak to beak? He's Coguillant de Mautirec. And by them, see the two on dappled horses, bearing a lion sable? One is called Semiramis [sic] and the other is his companion; they've painted their shields alike. And see the knight [5800] whose device is a gate, and a hart issuant therefrom? That, upon my word, is King Yder."

So ran the talk in the gallery: "That shield was made in Limoges, and Pilades brought it from there, who was starving to be in the tournament. And that one was made in Toulouse, and the breast-plate and harness-mountings too; the Count of Estrau brought it. That one is from Lyon-on-the-Rhône: there's none so good under the throne. For great merit it was bestowed on Taulas of the Desert, who carries it well and covers

14. Heraldic terms: "gules a bend or" is red with a gold stripe from the bearer's right shoulder to his left hip; "parti vert and azure" is half green, half blue.

himself with it nicely. The other shield is English work, made in London, where you see those two martlets looking as if they were about to take off—but they're not moving: they're staying to take blows with steel of Poitou. Young Thoas bears that device."

So they talked, blazoning the arms of those they recognized. But they saw nothing of the man they had scorned so much. They thought he had taken himself off, when he did not join the tournament.

When the Queen did not see him, she got the notion of sending to search the lines until he should be found. She could think of no better person to hunt for him than the girl she had sent to him the day before. At once she called her: "Go, Damsel, mount your palfrey. I'm sending you to the same knight as yesterday. Search till you find him: don't stop for anything. And then tell him again that 'poor little' is his instructions. When you have told him, pay close attention to his answer."

The girl did not delay. The previous evening she had taken care to note which direction he went, feeling certain she would be sent to him again. She set off through the lines until she saw him, then told him again that his fighting should be "poor-little" if he wanted the Queen's favor: the order came from her.

And he: "Since that is her command, tell her I thank her."

The maid left, and then the hooting began from the boys, servants, and squires. They cried, "There's a wonder: the knight in red armor has come back! But what's he doing? There's nothing in the world so base, so shameful, such a failure. Cowardice has him in her power and he can't do a thing against her."

The maiden rode back to the Queen, who held her very short and close until she heard the answer, which pleased her very much: now she knew beyond a doubt that this was the knight to whom she belonged, and he to her, unmistakably. She told the damsel to hurry back and tell him his orders were "the best" he could. She replied that she would go right back without a rest. From the grandstand she ran down to where her boy was waiting with her horse. Mounting, she rode off until she found the knight, and hastened to tell him, "Now, Sir, my Lady tells you, 'the best you can.'"

He answered, "Tell her there is nothing I mind doing if she wants it: whatever pleases her suits me."

She was prompt to carry back his message, which she knew would delight the Queen. She rode back as fast as she could to the gallery, [5900] and the Queen stood up and stepped to meet her, not going down the stairs, but waiting at the top. Up came the maid, happy to deliver her message. She started up the stairs, and reaching the Queen said, "Madam, I never saw a knight so courteous that he would so absolutely follow anything you told him. If you want the truth, he seems just as happy over the good orders as the bad."

"Indeed," answered the Queen, "it may well be." And she returned to her window to watch the knights.

Lancelot, without delay, took his shield by the grips, burning to show all his prowess. He turned his horse's head and ran it between two lines. Soon now the misguided mockers who teased him part of the previous day and overnight would be cheered up. They had been having their fun at his expense for quite a while.

The king's son of Ireland gripped his shield by the arm-straps and spurred furiously toward him from the opposite direction. They struck together so hard that the Irish prince felt no further desire for jousting: his lance was shattered, for he had not struck moss, but tough, seasoned planking. Lancelot had taught him one of his tricks in that joust; for he squeezed his shield to his arm and his arm to his side and bore him off his horse.

At once knights broke loose, spurring from each side, some to relieve him and others to hinder. Some, intending to aid their lords, emptied quite a few saddles in the ensuing mêlée. But never that whole day did Gawain take arms, though he was there with the others. He was too happy watching the feats of the knight in gules, which he thought outshone all the others'.

And the herald regained his spirits to the point of crying out in everyone's hearing, "Here's the man will take their measure! This very day you'll see what he does: this very day his worth will be shown."

Turning his horse, Lancelot spurred toward an elegant knight with a blow which landed him a hundred feet or more beyond his horse. He began fighting so well with sword and lance that none who bore arms could watch him without pleasure. Indeed, the knights present were delighted, for it was a joy to watch him knocking down horses and knights together. Hardly a knight he met remained in his saddle. The horses he won he gave to any who wanted them.

Those who had been teasing him said, "We're shamed and dead! How wrong we were to despise him and hold him cheap: he's really worth a thousand of the others in this field. He has outfought all the knights in the world: not one can compare with him."

And the maidens, gazing at him in wonder, said he was beyond their marrying. Not one was so confident in her beauty, her riches, her power or her rank as to conceive that beauty or fortune [6000] made her worthy of that knight, he was so brave. And yet most of them vowed to themselves that if they could not marry him, they would not marry this year, nor be given to any lord or husband.

The Queen, listening to their pledges, laughed at them inside; she knew that if all the gold of Araby were set before him, he would not take the best of them, the noblest nor the most beautiful, this man who so pleased them all.

They, with a single will, all wanted him, and one was as jealous of another as if she were already his wife. They saw him so skillful and were so pleased with him that they thought no one could fight like him. He fought so well that when the tournament broke up, both sides declared the knight of the red shield had no peer. Everyone said it, and it was true.

But as he left, he dropped his shield in the thickest of the press, and also his lance and shield-cover [cloak?], then galloped off. He rode off so fast that not a soul in the group noticed. Lancelot set out straight for where he had come from, to fulfill his oath. As the tournament ended, everyone looked and enquired for him, but they could not find him, for he was on his way, not wanting to be recognized.

The knights were extremely sorry, for they would have celebrated him to the skies, could they have kept him. And if the knights were downcast that he had left them, even more heavy-hearted were the maidens when they found out. By Saint John, they said, they would not marry this year. If they could not have the man they wanted, they would dismiss all the others. So the tournament was broken up without anyone's taking a husband.

Lancelot, without lingering, returned to his captivity. The seneschal had got home two or three days before, and asked where Lancelot was. The lady, who had lent Lancelot his well-furbished red armor, his harness, and his horse, told the seneschal the truth: she had sent him to fight in the Poore-Lyttel tournament.

"Honestly, Lady, you could not have done worse! I shall have great harm from this, I fear. My Lord Meleagant will treat me worse than the giant if I'd been shipwrecked.[15] I'll be dead, I'll be banished, as soon as he finds out. He'll never have mercy on me."

"My dear Lord, don't worry, don't be so afraid: there's no need. Nothing can keep him away, for he swore to me on relics that he would come back, so he can't do anything else."

The seneschal mounted, rode to his lord and told him all that had happened. But Meleagant reassured him when the seneschal told him how his wife had taken Lancelot's oath to return to prison. "He'll never break his oath," Meleagant told him, "I know it. Still, I am pained by what your wife has done. I wouldn't for anything have had him at that tournament. But now go back home, and when he comes, see [6100] that he's kept in a prison he can't get out of, with no freedom of movement. Then report to me."

"Your orders shall be carried out," said the seneschal, and left. He found Lancelot returned to captivity in his house. A messenger dispatched by the seneschal hurried straight back to Meleagant to tell him Lancelot had come. Hearing this, the prince got masons and carpenters who, reluctantly or gladly, would do what he told them. He sent for the best in the country and ordered them to build a tower, and work hard to finish it

---

15. "Giant." Cyclops, presumably, who wanted to eat the shipwrecked Ulysses.

quickly. It was to be by the sea, with the stone ferried to it: for by the kingdom of Gorre a wide estuary ran in, with an island in the middle which Meleagant knew well. He had the stone and timber for the tower carried there. It was all finished in fifty-seven days, strong and thick and high and wide.

Once it was built, he had Lancelot brought and put inside the tower. Then he ordered all the doors mortared shut, and had all the masons swear they would never say a word of the place. He intended it to be kept secret, and left no door or entrance but one little window. There Lancelot had to stay, and the food they gave him was poor and scanty, sent through the little window I just mentioned. Those were the orders of that vicious traitor Meleagant. Having accomplished what he wanted, he hurried straight to King Arthur's court.[16]

Arriving, he came before the King, full of overweening pride, and spoke thus: "King, I have undertaken a combat before you and all your household, but I don't see a trace of Lancelot, my opponent. Still, as is right, in the hearing of all, I hereby present my challenge before all here. If Lancelot is present, let him come forward and be man enough to keep in your court the promise he made me a year ago today. I don't know if anyone ever told you how this battle was set up, but I see knights here who were there when we made our pledges, and they could tell you if they wanted to report the truth. But if he tries to refuse me, I won't hire soldiers, I'll show him man to man."

Guinevere, seated beside the King, drew him toward her and said, "My Lord, do you know who this is? It's Meleagant, who abducted me and took Kay the Seneschal and hurt and shamed him."

The King answered, "Lady, I heard: I know this is the man who held my people captive."

16. About here, Godfrey de Leigni takes over from Chrétien.

She said no more. Arthur addressed Meleagant: "Friend, so help me God, we do not know any news of Lancelot, which saddens us."

"Sir King," answered Meleagant, "Lancelot told me I should find him here without fail. I was to utter this challenge nowhere but in your court. I want all these lords present to bear me witness that I summon him for a year from today, by our promise [6200] when we first arranged this combat."

At that Lord Gawain jumped up, stung by Meleagant's words, and cried, "Sir, Lancelot is not even in this country. But we will send to look for him, and God willing someone will find him before the year is out, if he isn't dead or captured. And if he doesn't come, give me the battle: I will fight it. I'll arm for Lancelot that day, if he doesn't get here sooner."

"Hah! Good King, for God's sake, give it him," cried Meleagant. "He wants it, and I request it, for I don't know a knight in the world I'd rather measure myself against, except only Lancelot. But know this: if one of those two doesn't fight me, I'll take no substitutes except one of them."

Arthur granted that, if Lancelot did not appear first. So Meleagant left his court and never stopped until he found his father, King Bademagu. Before him, to look like a worthy knight, Meleagant began a terrific charade. That day the King was holding court merrily in his city of Bath. It was his birthday, so he held a full court; crowds of diverse people had assembled with him. The palace was thronged with knights and maidens.

But there was one of them — Meleagant's sister — of whom I plan to tell you more, but not here, since it is not germane to my present subject. I'm not going to maim or rape her, but lead her by a straight, safe path.

But now I shall tell you that Meleagant arrived and in the

hearing of great and small cried, "Father, on your salvation, please tell me: shouldn't the knight rejoice, isn't the knight valiant, who by his arms makes himself feared in King Arthur's court?"

His father, without waiting for more, answered, "Son, all good people should honor and serve the knight who could do that, and spend time in his company." Then he spoke affectionately to him, and begged him not to hide why he had brought up the subject, what he was looking for, what he wanted, and where he came from.

"Sir," answered his son, "I don't know if you remember the pledges taken and recorded when you made peace between Lancelot and me. I expect you do remember that before witnesses, we were told that both of us were to be ready a year from that day in Arthur's court. I went there when I was supposed to, armed and ready for my errand. I did all my duty: asked for Lancelot, whom I was pitted against. But I couldn't find him anywhere; he had fled!

"I left with this understanding: Gawain gave his word that if Lancelot is dead or doesn't arrive within the set time, he's promised me there will be no more delay, but Gawain himself will fight me instead of Lancelot. Arthur has no knight so highly praised as him, it's well known. [6300] But before the elders bloom, I'll see, if we get to blows, whether his reputation fits his deeds. I wish it were now."

"Son," retorted his father, "you are making a fool of yourself. Now anyone who didn't know will learn your folly from your own lips. The truth is that a good heart humbles itself, but the overweening fool will never be rid of his folly. I'm saying this for you, Son, because you are such a hard, dry person with no sweetness or friendship. Your heart lacks all mercy: you are too in love with folly. That's why I scorn you; that's what will drag you down. If you are a worthy knight, there will be enough witnesses to it when you need them. A brave man does not praise his own courage to boast of his deeds: the deed praises itself. Your own praise doesn't increase your reputation by a lark's weight — I actually esteem you less for it.

"Son, I lecture you, but what good does it do? Words are wasted on a fool: trying to argue a fool out of his folly only gets one beaten. Good teaching is worth nothing if it's not put into practice; rather, it's lost and gone."

At that, Meleagant was beside himself. I can assure you, you've never seen any mother's son so full of rage. By his anger, the family truce was broken then and there, for he would no longer be polite to his father, but said, "Are you dreaming, to say I'm wrong when I tell you about myself? I thought I was coming to you as my lord and as my father — but it doesn't look that way. You're insulting me, I think, worse than you should, and you can't give me one reason for lighting into me like that."

"Oh, yes I can."

"What, then?"

"Because I can see nothing in you but raving madness. I know your character very well, and it will ruin you yet. Curse whoever believes that Lancelot, that well-brought-up man, praised by everybody but you, would have fled for fear of you. More likely he's run into a prison with doors so tight he can't get out without permission. Note that I should be extremely angry if he were dead or harmed. It would be a great loss if such a gifted creature, so beautiful, so brave, so self-possessed, had died so soon — but that's not so, God willing."

Bademagu said no more. But a maiden daughter of his had heard every word he uttered. Know that she was the one I mentioned before, and she was not happy to hear such news of Lancelot. She realized that he was being concealed, since not a word of him had transpired. She said, "May God never look kindly on me if I rest until I find out certain news of him."

So without delay and without a sound she ran off to mount a mule, a pretty one with a smooth gait. But I can tell you she had no notion which way to turn on leaving the court. Having no leads, she turned into the first road she found, and hurried along at random, without knight or squire. [6400] She hastened in her eagerness to find what she sought; she exhausted herself with hunting, but it was not to be so soon. She could not rest, nor pause long anywhere, anxious to achieve her intent: getting Lancelot out of prison, if she could and if she found him. But I think that before finding him, she will have searched many countries through and through before hearing any news of him. Why should I report her travels or stops?

She traveled so many roads, up and down, hither and yon, that a month or more had passed without her learning any more than she knew before: nothing. One day, heavy-hearted, she was riding across a field, and far off by the shore of an arm of the sea she noticed a tower; but for a league around it was no house, hut, or shelter. Meleagant had had it made to put Lancelot in, but the girl knew nothing of it. As soon as she saw it, she fixed it with an unswerving gaze. Her heart promised her that here was the thing she had hunted for so long. Now she had fulfilled her quest, for Fortune, having led her such a long road, had led her to the right one at last.

The maiden approached the tower close enough to touch it. She went round it, listening to be sure whether she could hear any hopeful sound. She looked down, she craned upward, she saw the tower was high and thick. But she wondered at seeing neither door nor window, except one little narrow one. On all that tall, straight tower was no stairway nor ladder. She reasoned that it had been made so on purpose, and that Lancelot was inside; and before a morsel passed her lips, she would know if it were true or not.

So then she called him by name. She wanted to summon Lancelot, but she was getting impatient by the time she heard, as she paused, a voice lamenting in that strange, strong tower: a voice desiring only death. It longed for death, it mourned exceedingly: its pain was too great, it wanted to die. It hated its life, it hated itself, and it rasped feebly, "Oh, Fortune, what a bad turn your wheel has given me! You've spun it cruelly, for I was at the top and now I'm at the bottom: I was well-placed, now badly; now I weep — I used to laugh. Alas, miserable man, why did you laugh, when Fortune has deserted you so soon. In such a short time she has thrown me from high to low. Fortune, you were wrong to fool me, but what do you care? It makes no difference to you how things go. Oh, holy cross, Holy Ghost, how lost I am: I am finished.

"Oh, Gawain, so good a knight (how I ramble),[17] there's not your equal in kindness; I certainly am puzzled why you don't rescue me. Indeed, you're taking too long, which is not courteous. I, who have always been your good friend, should

17. "(How I ramble)." This is the way Roques prints the lines from Guiot's manuscript, and he mentions no other MS writing it differently. However, the passage would flow better and (I think) make better sense if lines 6483 and 6484 were reversed, yielding

con sui perduz, con sui periz,
con sui del tot en tot alez!
Ha! Gauvain, vos qui tant valez,
qui de bontez n'avez paroil....

This would be translated: "how lost I am, how dead, how I have gone from one extreme to the other [happiness to misery, as he has just been saying]! Oh, Gawain, so worthy a knight, so unequaled in kindness....

have your help. On this side of the sea or beyond it, I can truly say, there would be no nook or cranny where I wouldn't have looked for you, at least seven years or ten, if I'd known you were captured, until I found you. But why do I keep on talking? [6500] You don't feel like going to the trouble. The peasants are right: more than one friend is hard to find. In need one can easily see who is a good friend.

"Alas, it's more than a year that I've been shut up in this tower. Gawain, I am insulted at your leaving me here. But maybe you don't know: I might be blaming you unjustly. Yes, that's so, I feel sure, and I was wrong and unfair to think what I did. I'm convinced that for everything under the clouds you wouldn't have neglected to come with your men and get me out of these straits, had you known about it. Indeed, you should, for friendship and fellowship, and I'll never say otherwise. But that's nothing, it can't be.

"Oh, God and Saint Sylvester curse the man who's put me to such shame! He's the worst creature alive, Meleagant, who has done me all the harm he can, out of envy." With that he stopped speaking, that knight who was wearing away his life in sorrow.

But the maiden, attentive at the foot of the tower, had heard every word. Waiting no longer, since she knew she had reached her goal, she shouted to him as loud as she could, "Lancelot!" adding, "Friend, up there, speak to a friend of yours!"

But he, inside, did not hear her. She forced herself to shout louder and louder, until the knight in his weakened state half heard, and wondered who could be calling him. Her voice came in, he heard himself hailed, but did not know who it was; a phantom, he thought.

He looked all round, to see if he could see anyone, but saw nothing but the tower and himself. "God, what do I hear? I hear talking but see nothing! Faith, this is more than strange; and I'm not asleep, but awake. I suppose if I'd had a dream I'd think it wasn't true; but I'm awake, and that bothers me."

With some difficulty he got up and started toward the little hole, gingerly, step by step. Reaching it, he leaned into the embrasure and looked up, down, and from side to side. Gazing out as hard as he could, he caught sight of the girl who had hailed him. He did not recognize her, but he saw her.

As for her, she recognized him at once, and said, "Lancelot, I've come a long way looking for you, and now it's happened, thank God, I've found you. I'm the girl who asked you a favor on your way to the Sword-bridge, and you willingly granted it: the head of the defeated knight, which I had you cut off, for I was not at all fond of him. For that favor and service I have gone to all this trouble: for I will get you out of there."

"Thank you, Damsel," answered the prisoner. "My favor will be well repaid if I'm to get out of here. If you can get me out, I can truly promise that I will be yours henceforth, so help me Saint Paul the Apostle; and, so may I meet God face to face, there will never be a day when I won't do anything you please to command. There's nothing you could ask of me, provided I had it, that wouldn't be yours on the spot."

"Friend, never doubt but you'll escape: this very day you shall be set free. [6600] I would not leave you in there till tomorrow for a thousand pounds. And then I'll give you a good rest and some real comfort. Anything I have that you like, if you want it, it's yours. Don't worry about a thing. First I've got to get hold (wherever it may be) of some tool to enlarge that hole with, if I can find one, so you can get out."

"God grant you find it," agreed Lancelot. "In here I've got plenty of rope, which the servants gave me to pull up my food: hard barley-bread and muddy water, which has been making me sick."

Then Bademagu's daughter found a strong, square, sharp pick, and quickly gave it to Lancelot, who hewed and struck, hit and smote — difficult though it was for him — until he could easily get out. Then he was relieved, then he was happy, you may be sure, when he was drawn from his prison and left the place where he had been mewed up for so long. Now he was free, now he was soaring. Know that for all the gold spread round the world, piled into one mountain and offered to him, he would not have wanted to be back there.

Now Lancelot was set free, so starved that he staggered with hunger and weakness. Gently, so as not to hurt him, the girl set him in front of her on the mule and galloped away. But she left the road, on purpose so no one would see them. They rode in cover, because if she had traveled in the open, probably someone she knew would soon have harmed them, and she did not want that. Thus she avoided dangers and arrived at a retreat where she often stayed, because it was a beautiful and kindly place. The house and its people were entirely at her orders, and the site was planted all round, healthy and very private.

There Lancelot arrived. At once, when he was stripped of his gown, the maiden laid him softly on a beautiful high couch, bathed him, and took such good care of him that I could not tell you half of it. Gently she rubbed him down and outfitted him, as she would have her father. She restored him completely, renewed him and changed all his clothes. Now he was as beautiful as an angel, no longer starved or pining, but strong and handsome. He rose. And the damsel fetched him the most beautiful robe she could find, to put on when he got up.

Gladly he donned it, lighter than a bird on the wing. He embraced and kissed the maid and kindly said, "My friend, I thank only God and you for my healing. You have set me free from prison: for that you may take my heart and me, my service and my fortune for your own whenever you wish. You have done so much for me that I am your man. But it's a long time since I have been at the court of my Lord King Arthur, who has done me great honor; and there will be things for me to do there. So, my dear and gracious friend, I would beg permission of your love to go there, and if you were willing, I should be glad to be on my way."

"Lancelot, my dear, fair friend, I'm willing," answered the girl, "for I desire your honor and your good in every place." [6700] She gave him a wonderful horse she had, the best ever seen. He jumped on, asking leave of no stirrups — one could hardly tell how he had got up. Then they affectionately commended each other to God Who never lies.

Lancelot set out, so happy that I could not, even if I'd sworn to, tell you of his joy at being thus escaped from his trap. But now he rode along reiterating that it was that misbegotten traitor's unlucky hour when he held him prisoner. Now the trick was on him, "for I'm free in spite of him." And he swore on the heart and body of Him Who made the world that not for all the riches from Babylon to Ghent would he let Meleagant go if he caught and defeated him, for he had maltreated and shamed Lancelot too grievously.

But the time of reckoning was coming, for that Meleagant whom Lancelot was threatening with such short shrift had arrived at court that very day, uninvited. When he got there, he demanded Sir Gawain until he got him. Then Meleagant asked about Lancelot, whether that proven traitor had been seen or found, as though he knew nothing about him. And in fact he didn't: Meleagant did not know where Lancelot was, though he thought he did. Gawain told him the truth: that he had not seen him, nor had he come back.

"Seeing that's the case and I've found you," said Meleagant, "come on and keep my compact, for I won't wait for you any longer."

Gawain retorted, "I'll keep your compact, God willing, soon enough. I can deal with you. But if it comes to throwing for high points and I throw more than you, so help me God and Saint Faith, I won't hesitate to pocket the entire stake."

Without further delay Gawain ordered a rug spread before him. His squires, unafraid, quickly obeyed his orders: with no grumbling they set about doing as he asked: taking the carpet and laying it where he said. He jumped on without pausing and ordered the nearest youths to arm him, though they were still not dressed themselves. There were three of them, Gawain's cousins or maybe nephews,[18] anyway well-brought-up and brave lads. They armed him so well that nobody could have found a detail to correct in their work. After arming him, one of them fetched a Spanish charger, swifter in running over field and wood, hill and dale, than the good Bucephalus himself.[19]

Onto that horse mounted the famous knight Gawain, the best-trained who ever received a blessing. He was just about to take his shield when he saw Lancelot dismounting before

18. "Cousins or nephews." Readers of later Arthurian material will see these three lads as Gawain's brothers Agravaine, Gaheris and Gareth, even if Loomis has shown that the multiplication of G-names is a confusion from Gawain himself.

19. "Bucephalus." Alexander the Great's horse.

him — Lancelot, whom he had not expected. With astonishment he stared at him, arrived so suddenly. To tell the truth, Gawain was as amazed as if Lancelot had fallen from the clouds before his eyes. But when he was assured that it was truly he, nothing could have kept him from jumping to the ground; he ran toward him with outstretched arms, hugged him, greeted him, and kissed him. [6800] Now Gawain was happy, now he was relieved, to have found his friend. And it's a fact, believe me, that Gawain at that point would not have been chosen King if it had meant parting with Lancelot.

Now King Arthur knew, and everybody, that Lancelot, in spite of all, Lancelot, whom they had missed for so long, had arrived safe and sound. Everyone rejoiced, and the court gathered to celebrate him, which had lacked him for so long. Nobody, old or young, but was glad of him. Their joy shattered and erased their former sorrow: mourning fled and gladness appeared, rousing them.

And the Queen? Wasn't she among the general rejoicing? Yes indeed, in the forefront. What? Heavens, where was she, then? She had never been so happy as now, at his safe arrival, and did she not go to him? Indeed, she came so close to it that her body very nearly followed her heart. And where was the heart? Kissing and welcoming Lancelot. Then why was her body hidden? Wasn't it full of joy? Was there any anger or hate in it? No, not a crumb. But maybe there was something: the King and the others there with wide-open eyes might perceive how things stood, if in front of everybody she had done all her heart wished. If Reason could not rid her of that madness, they would see exactly how she felt, and that would have been

insanity indeed. So Reason bound up her wild heart and out-
rageous thoughts, talked some sense into her, and put it off
until she should discover some better, more private place than
they had just then.

The King did Lancelot great honor, and when he had finished welcoming him, said, "Friend, I've had no news of anyone
for a long time which pleased me so much as this of you. But
I do wonder where, in what country, you could have been for
so long. All winter and all summer I've had you searched for
high and low, but nobody could find you."

"Indeed, my Lord, I can tell you soon enough what happened to me. Meleagant was holding me, the vicious traitor,
in prison, from the time the captives were set free from his
land. He kept me living shamefully in a tower by the sea: there
he had me shut up, and there I'd still be dragging out a miserable life if it hadn't been for a friend of mine, a maiden I'd done
a small favor for once. She, for a negligible gift, gave me a great
reward, and did me great honor and great good. But that
knight, whom I declare my enemy, who did me such an ill turn
and heaped such shame on me—I want to pay him back right
now. He's come for his payment and he shall have it: he mustn't
wait any longer. It's too close. And I'm ready. But God forbid
he should ever boast of his reward."

Gawain said to Lancelot, "Friend, that reward—if I pay off
your creditor, it won't be so big a favor. Here I am all mounted
and ready, as you see. Dear friend, don't refuse me this favor,
I beg!"

[6900] Lancelot retorted that he'd have an eye torn out, or
both, before Gawain would persuade him to that. He swore it

should never happen: he owed Meleagant and he would pay him, for he had pledged it with his own hand.

Gawain saw that anything he could say was no use. So he stripped off his hauberk and disarmed completely. Lancelot armed himself in the same gear straightway; already he could envision the time when he would have avenged himself.

Meleagant would never thrive again, but get his just deserts. He was beside himself with astonishment at the wonder before his eyes; he came close to losing his mind. "I was a real fool not to go and check, before I came here, that I still had him imprisoned in my tower. Now he's tricked me. But, good God, why should I have gone? How, for what reason, should I have thought he might have escaped? Isn't the wall built thick enough, and the tower strong and high? And there was no door, no crack he could have got out of, unless he had outside help. Maybe someone found out he was there. Or, suppose the walls were rotten and fell in, wouldn't he have fallen too, and be dead and dismembered and broken? Yes, so help me, completely, if he'd fallen, he'd be dead for sure. Besides, I think that when that wall falls, the whole sea will run away and not leave a drop, and the mountain will no longer stand — unless my tower were knocked down by force.

"There's some other way. He had help when he got out, and didn't fly out without it. I'm made a fool of by a conspiracy. Whatever happened, he's out. If I'd taken proper precautions, it would never have happened and he would never have reached this court. But it's too late to regret that. The peasants, no liars, have a valid proverb: it's too late to lock the barn after the horse is stolen. Now I shall be treated shamefully if I can't take it. Take what? What suffering? Well, as long as I last I'll keep him busy, please God, in Whom I put my trust."

So he comforted himself and asked only that they be put in

the field together. And soon they will be, I do believe, for Lancelot is coming looking for him, in hopes of dispatching him quickly. But before they attacked each other, the King told both to go down to a field below the tower; there was not so pretty a one from there to Ireland. So down they rode as ordered, and promptly. The King also went there, and all the men and women by crowds and throngs: everyone went, no one stayed behind. And to the windows crowded many knights, ladies, and maidens, noble and fair, for Lancelot's sake.

In the field grew a sycamore, the loveliest that could be. It spread out wide, and all round it grew short cool grass, fresh in every season. From under this beautiful great sycamore, planted in Abel's time, sprang a clear, rapid streamlet. Its pebbles were bright and pretty as silver, and its bed as smelted refined gold. It ran down the middle of the meadow in the valley between two woods. There the King was pleased to sit, [7000] finding nothing to discommode him. He had the spectators stand well back up the slope, and Lancelot rushed upon Meleagant with the fury of a man who has all cause for hatred.

But before striking him, Lancelot cried fiercely, "Come on, I defy you! Be sure I won't spare you!" Then he spurred his horse and moved back a bowshot. Then they let their horses charge at full gallop. Both struck each other on their stout shields and pierced them through, but neither fighter was wounded at that point. Without stopping they galloped past each other, then turned to strike again, as hard as their horses could go, at those good strong shields. Both the knights, brave and noble, and the horses, strong and fleet, were fit for that heavy fighting.

By their great blows, their lances passed unbroken through the shields round their necks and thrust through to the bare skin. The strength of each knight's blow bore the other to the ground: not chest-strap, girth, nor stirrup was of any help. Each flew backward from his saddle and fell to the bare ground. The horses, in fright, ran off over hill and dale, one kicking, the other biting, trying to kill each other.

The fallen knights jumped up as fast as they could and whipped out their inscribed swords. They held their shields before their faces and devoted their attention to damaging each other with the keen steel. Lancelot had no fear of Meleagant, for he knew half again as much swordsmanship; he had learned it as a child. They exchanged heavy blows to their shields and gold-barred helmets, breaking and bending them. But Lancelot pressed Meleagant until he got in a heavy blow in front of his shield on his mailed right arm, and cut it off. As Meleagant felt himself hurt, losing his right hand, he said it would be dearly sold. If he could get no breathing-space, he would wait for nothing. His pain and anger were so great he nearly ran mad, and thought no more of his own state, only of harming Lancelot. He rushed at him, intending to grapple with him, but Lancelot defended himself and with his sharp sword gave Meleagant such a gash in the vitals that he would never recover till April or May. He rammed his nasal into his teeth hard enough to cave in three.

Meleagant was too enraged to utter a word, nor deigned to sue for mercy; for his mad heart, too much his tyrant, told him not to. Lancelot came up, unlaced his helmet, and cut off his head. Meleagant will never get away: he is dead and done for. And I can tell you that of all the people who saw it, not one felt sorry for him: the King and all the spectators rejoiced. They disarmed Lancelot, making more of him than ever, and led him home in great joy.

Lords, if I told any more, it would be outside my story, so I shall stop here. This is the end of the romance.

The clerk Godfrey de Leigny has finished *The Cart;* but let nobody blame him for working on Chrétien's story, for he did it with the permission of Chrétien who began it. Godfrey wrote it from the part where Lancelot was walled up to the end of the story. So far he has written, and he will put neither more nor less, for either would spoil the tale.

The end of the Romance of Lancelot in the Cart.

Selected Bibliography

There is an excellent bibliography of the literature on Chrétien de Troyes: Douglas Kelly, *Chrétien de Troyes: An Analytic Bibliography* (London, 1976). It is very well organized by topics and lists all important material up to the date of publication.

The books listed below are general studies of the poet's work or of *Lancelot* in particular. Some of them have appeared since the publication of Kelly's bibliography.

Cross, T.P., and W.A. Nitze. *Lancelot and Guenevere: A Study on the Origins of Courtly Love.* Chicago, 1930; repr. New York, 1970.

Frappier, J. *Chrétien de Troyes: l'homme et l'oeuvre.* Paris, 1957. Frequently reprinted.

Haidu, P. *Aesthetic Distance in Chrétien de Troyes: Irony and Comedy in "Cligés and "Perceval."* Geneva, 1968. (Many of the arguments advanced are equally applicable to *Lancelot.*)

Kelly, D. *"Sens" and "Conjointure" in the "Chevalier de la Charrette."* The Hague, 1966.

Loomis, R.S. *Arthurian Literature in the Middle Ages.* Oxford, 1959.

———*Arthurian Tradition and Chrétien de Troyes*. New York, 1949.

Owen, D.D.R. "Chrétien de Troyes." In *European Authors*, vol. 3, Middle Ages. Ed. W.T.H. Jackson. New York, 1983.

Ribard, J. *Chrétien de Troyes, Le Chevalier de la Charrette; essai d'interprétation symbolique*. Paris, 1972.

Topsfield, L.T. *Chrétien de Troyes: a Study of the Arthurian Romances*. Cambridge and New York, 1981.